BRANDER'S ORIGINAL GUIDE TO
SCOTCH WHISKY

To
Ed Zern
Transatlantic Sportsman and Literary Critic
Who assessed some fine malt whiskies with me
(v. Glossary p.172)

BRANDER'S ORIGINAL GUIDE TO

Scotch Whisky

MICHAEL BRANDER

illustrated by Rosamund Fowler

THE GLENEIL PRESS

The first Definitive Guide to
Scotch Whisky
Over 25 years old and still going strong

First published in 1975 by
Johnston & Bacon, Publishers
Regularly re-printed and up-dated
First revised edition published in 1990 by
Canongate Publishing Ltd,
second revised edition published
in 1992 by Canongate Press plc
New revised edition published in 1995 by
The Gleneil Press.
Reprinted 1995
This completely revised edition
published in 2000 by
The Gleneil Press
Whittingehame Haddington, EH41 4QA

British Library Cataloguing in
Publication Data
A catalogue record is available for this book
from the British Library
Brander, Michael
Brander's Original Guide to Scotch Whisky.
5 Rev. ed.

ISBN 0-9525330-7-3
Typeset by Hewer Text Limited, Edinburgh
Printed and bound by Omnia Books Ltd, Glasgow

Contents

Foreword

In 1974 Michael Brander wrote *A History of Scotch Whisky, The Original Scotch*, which gained the Glenfiddich Award for the Malt Whisky Book Author of the Year. This was followed in 1975 by *A Guide to Scotch Whisky*, published by Johnston & Bacon of Edinburgh. After numerous reprintings this only went out of print in the late 1980s with the demise of the old established firm. Meanwhile, in 1982, he had written a short *Introduction to Scotch Whisky*, published by Holmes McDougal. In 1990 the essentials of these three books were combined in *The Essential Guide to Scotch Whisky*, published by Canongate Publishing Ltd. In 1992 a revised second edition was published by Canongate Press, who went into Receivership in 1994. A new and freshly up-dated revised second edition of the Guide which had been selling steadily for twenty years was published in 1995 by the Gleneil Press, re-titled, *The Original Guide to Scotch Whisky* In 1996 another edition was published in the USA by Lyons & Burford entitled *Brander's Guide to Scotch Whisky*, re-printed 1998. In 2000 the Gleneil Press have now published a further new, revised and up-dated edition re-titled *Brander's Original Guide to Scotch Whisky*.

This is intended as a basic guide to anyone interested in Scotch whisky. There is a brief introduction to the origins of Scotch from the earliest days to the present, showing how the drink is essentially a product of Scotland's barley, water and peat as well as the inherited skills of the distillers, which have passed down the centuries. The years when Scotch whisky was produced illegally because of crushing taxation are also briefly outlined. Then came the boom years of the last century when Scotch whisky was first sold all round the world. These were followed by the lean years of the two world wars until finally the post 1945 period was reached.

Michael Brander demonstrates how in the half century that followed foreign investment was not always a good thing, resulting too often in mergers between ever-larger financial corporations totally unconnected to the Scotch whisky industry with subsequent accountancy 'rationalisations' during each successive take-over followed by distilleries changing hands and the consequent destablisation of an industry which depends very greatly on continuity, long term planning and investment, not only in finance but in the expertise and personal commitment of its' employees. He also points out how by using it as a milch cow for excessive taxation successive governments themselves have damaged Scotland's greatest industry by exasercbating these trends. He goes on to show how patent-still grain whisky is made and how this differs crucially from pot-still malt distilling. He then delineates the art of the blender and from that indicates how Scotch whisky, whether blended or malt, should be drunk for maximum enjoyment and personal satisfaction (see D.I.Y., p. 37). After this brief but illuminating introduction, in the major part of the book he goes through Scotland's malt distilleries alphabetically, indicating their whereabouts, their background, their present owners and the quality of their product. In the Almanack of Distilling Events which follows he notes important events in the history of Scotch Whisky including details of the major financial mergers and take-overs in the industry. He concludes with a list of Vatted Malts and Malt Whisky merchants, as well as a Glossary of Technical Terms and a bibliography. Even those who think they know their Scotch whisky will find something of value in these pages and for those who wish to learn about Scotch whisky here, devoid of frills, but with all that anyone needs know, is the perfect pocket introduction.

Acknowledgements

My grateful thanks and acknowledgements once again are owed to very many people throughout the Scotch whisky industry for the ready and willing assistance. It is perhaps invidious to single out individuals and understandably enough many prefer not to be mentioned at all, but once again I must place on record how very helpful everyone whom I have approached has been, from the Scotch Whisky Association downwards. In particular I would like to thank the many un-named distillers and distillery workers who have invariably been very helpful and courteous, as well as pleasant to meet. My thanks for their assistance over distillery details and in finding my way through the seemingly never-ending maze of closures and take-overs are due to many throughout the industry, but especially to Jim McLean at at Miltonduff and Silvia Waterson at the Dumbarton office of Allied Distillers, Denise Marshall, Richard Paterson and Elaine Bennett at JBB (Greater Europe) plc., Colin Ross at Ben Nevis Distillery, Raymond Armstrong at Bladnoch Distillery, Robin Dodds at Burn Stewart, Vanessa Wright at Campbell Distillers, Neil Boyd at John Dewar, Terry Hillman at Angus Dundee Distillers, Malcolm Cannon at Edrington, Barbara Nimmo at Glenmorangie, Ian Urquhart at Gordon & MacPhail, John Grant at Glenfarclas, Elizabeth Lafferty and David Mair at Wm Grant & Sons, Jacqui Stacey at Inver House Distillers, Paul Garwood, Isle of Arran Distillers, Henry Jagielko at Loch Lomond Distillery Co., Ltd., Derek Gilchrist at Morrison Bowmore, Yvonne Thackeray and Iain Russell, archivist, at Seagram Distillers, Stuart Hendry at Speyside, Frank McHardy at Springbank, Jim Milne at Tomatin, Robet Fleming at Tomintoul, Ken Robertson and archivist Christine Jones at UDV, Andrew McDonald and Mrs McEwan at the Scotch Whisky Heritage Centre, also my

ix

old friends Ross Gunn, Mark Lawson and many others. I would also like to thank M. Thierry Chauvet, from Tahiti, who pointed out that in Mediaeval French, aqua vitae (p. 2 et seq) meant not 'water of life' as so often translated, but simply 'strong, or powerful, waters,' which having regard to the distilling standards of the day was more realistic. Finally, any opinions expressed are entirely my own and for any faults, omissions or mistakes I am entirely responsible.

The Background of Scotch Whisky

Scotland's Heritage

Scotch whisky may only legally be distilled in Scotland. Any bottles claiming to contain Scotch whisky which is not distilled in Scotland from Very Old Black and White Horses made in Chile to Finest Rising Sun Scotch Whisky or Whisaki made in Tokyo, are illegal imitations and the makers may be prosecuted. Scotch whisky has been made in Scotland for centuries, but regrettably the majority of Scots themselves know remarkably little about it, or about the art of distilling it. This is a part of the national heritage about which there is still a widespread and lamentable ignorance, despite efforts from the 1980s onwards to remedy by measures such as the opening of distilleries as tourist attractions. forming a 'Whisky Trail' round the Highlands, the publication of numerous books on the subject and the opening of the Scotch Whisky Heritage Centre in Edinburgh. It must be appreciated, however, that Scotch whisky distilling, particularly the distilling of Scotch malt whisky in pot-stills, is not just another industry, and that Scotch whisky, especially Scotch malt whisky, is not just another drink, but that both are an integral part of Scotland itself. The pure air and water, the peat and the soil of Scotland, along with the inherited skills of the distillers themselves, combine magically in the making of Scotch whisky.

Origins

The elementary fact that alcohol boils at a lower temperature than water forms the basis of all distillation. Distilling is basically nothing more than boiling fermented liquor in a container. In primitive stills the steam is led off in a long tube, or condenser, like the elongated spout of a kettle. As the steam cools it reverts to liquid again in the form of alcohol which in such a simple still would contain lethal impurities as well. Like the invention of gunpowder, distilling probably originated in the Far East where the process may have started with primitive stills using bamboo and heating the juice of naturally fermented fruits.

Arrival in Britain

When the art of distilling first reached Britain is uncertain, but the making of ale from fermented malted barley, the first stage in the distilling of Scotch whisky, was known around the 6th century and possibly earlier. It has been suggested that St Patrick introduced the art of distilling to Scotland as early as the 5th century. Producing Scotch whisky from malted barley probably started a good deal later, possibly somewhere around the 11th or 12th centuries, by which time both the Scots and the Irish were undoubtedly experienced in the art of distilling spirits. It seems likely therefore that the Scots have known the art of distilling Scotch whisky for over a thousand years.

Aqua Vitae

In Europe, where fermented grapes in the shape of wine were readily available, the distillation of wine produced brandy, known as aqua vitae, or strong waters. In Scotland where fermented barley was the basis for ale, then the national drink, it would have been natural enough to use this as the basis for distilling, although the lees of wine were probably used at first. The use of fermented barley would have produced the earliest Scotch whisky, but at first, like brandy, this was also termed aqua vitae. It is thus difficult to say with any certainty when fermented barley was first used in place of wine, since in those early days there were no records of the distilling process.

First recorded use of malted barley

The earliest known record of malted barley being used instead of wine to make aqua vitae is in the Scottish Ex-

2

chequer Rolls dated 1494 and reads: "Eight bolls of malt to Friar John Cor, wherewith to make aqua vitae." As eight bolls amounts to half a ton of malt, enough to make around seventy gallons of spirit, it may be safely assumed that this was by no means the first time that Friar John Cor, or his fellow Friars, had made Scotch whisky, but that this was in fact an already long-established practice. However, though Scotch whisky had almost certainly been produced for many years in Scottish monasteries, since the spirit was generally referred to only as aqua vitae, it is impossible to be sure when the practice of using malted barley first started.

Origins of the name Whisky

It is as late as 1618 before the first mention may be found in an account of a chieftain's funeral in the Highlands of the drinking of *Uisge beatha*. This is the Gaelic for the Water of Life and the equivalent of aqua vitae. It was natural enough by degrees simply to refer to *Uisge*. Thereafter it was a very simple corruption of the Gaelic to arrive at the word Whisky.

The early distilling process

To judge by surviving illustrations the stills of the 15th and 16th centuries were primitive indeed. Although there are plenty of entries in the Exchequer Rolls to prove that the King of Scotland and his nobles were fond of whisky the spirit in those days must have been not only powerful, but also potentially lethal. Without accurate instruments for measuring quality and strength, it required great skill and practice to draw off the pure *middle cut* of the spirit and avoid the *foreshots*, or oily and poisonous higher alcohols at the start, and the later *feints* or *aftershots*, containing the lower alcohols at the end of the distilling process. During the 16th and 17th centuries the methods of distilling were steadily improved and over time it probably became a quite common domestic chore on farms with barley to spare, but even so it was not until the 18th century that distilling became really widespread in Scotland. Although the primitive 16th century stills probably held little more than thirty or forty gallons at most, by the mid-18th century stills holding several hundred

3

gallons were commonplace and distilling had become a science, an art and an industry.

Proof: The measurement of quality and strength

In these early stages gauging the quality and strength of spirit distilled was very rough and ready. One of the commoner methods was to set a measure alight and note how much was left. Another was to add a measure of gunpowder. If when lit it exploded this was considered too strong and *over proof*, but conversely if difficult to light it was considered weak and *under proof*. If it burned steadily it was considered the correct strength or *proof*. Then in 1675 Robert Boyle developed his instrument for comparing the specific gravities of liquids and 'Boyle's Bubble', although not accurate to a fine degree, was used to decide whether a spirit was below or above proof. It was over a hundred years before an improvement in this early hydrometer was introduced and even then it was erratic. Accurate gauging of proof was not achieved until 1818 when the government introduced a reliable hydrometer invented by an excise officer named Sikes. Under this spirit of proof strength at 51°F weighs 12/13ths of a similar quantity of distilled water.

The national drink

Until the Union of the Parliaments in 1707 ale, not whisky, was the national drink of Scotland. Ale was more popular by far with the mass of the population, especially in the Lowlands, than the then relatively expensive and less widely available spirit. While ale may have been the most popular drink with the bulk of the nation the upper classes, professional men and the aristocracy, tended to drink mainly claret, then readily obtainable from France. The imposition of a tax on malt in Scotland in 1725, contrary to the terms laid down in the Act of Union, resulted initially in widespread rioting and ultimately forced the brewers to raise the price of ale to cover their costs. It soon became apparent that a comparatively simple way to avoid the tax was to use the malted barley to distil whisky illicitly instead of making ale. A gradual change in the public taste resulted. By the end of

4

the 18th century whisky had replaced ale as the national drink. There was also the interesting side-effect towards the end of the 18th century that the Lowland distillers, distilling legally and paying tax on their malted barley, were forced to use quantities of unmalted barley to keep their costs down. Their whisky was thus naturally inferior to that of the Highland distillers who paid no tax and distilled their whisky illicitly.

Early Lowland distillers: Haig and Stein

At least one of the names subsequently to become prominent in the Scotch whisky industry had already been noted publicly in that connection as early as the latter half of the 17th century. A farming family named Hage at Throsk near Stirling were accused of distilling whisky on the Sabbath in the year 1655 and were summoned before the Kirk Session to be rebuked for their sins, but in the end their servant lass was held to blame. From the 18th century onwards the Haigs were to become one of the leading families in the Lowlands in the developing Scotch whisky industry there and went on, of course, to become one of the best known names in Scotch whisky right up to the present day. They intermarried with the Steins, another well-known Lowland distilling family of the late 18th and early 19th centuries. By the last quarter of the 18th century Robert and John Haig at Leith and James and John Stein at Clackmannan were using stills of over a thousand gallons capacity. To avoid the malt tax they used potatoes, turnips and other roots, or oats and wheat for distilling, using only small quantities of malted barley to aid the fermenting process. Although this spirit was much inferior to that produced from malted barley there was a great demand for the product in the highly populated Lowlands and they also exported it to England where it was refined into gin, even engaging in a deliberate trade war with the gin distillers in England.

Penal taxation: causes and effects

This competition from Scotland roused the anger of the powerful gin distillers' lobby in England. As a result of their pressures the government was persuaded to introduce what amounted to punitive taxation against the Scottish whisky distillers, basing this initially on the mistaken belief that a still could only be worked once in 24 hours. Ever increasing taxation from 1784 onwards and throughout the war with France led to ever increasing evasion and also to desperate measures to stay within the law. Ingenious Scottish distillers successfully distilled as much as eighty gallons of whisky in three and a half minutes, but naturally this tended to damage both the stills and the standard of whisky produced. The Haigs managed to survive, but the Steins, who had engaged in a cut-throat war with the southern distillers were forced into bankruptcy. As taxation still continued to rise under pressure from the English distillers, many Scots distillers were literally forced to turn to illegal distilling to survive.

The Highland Line

From the 1770s onwards distilling became more and more widespread in the Highlands, but still on a much smaller scale than in the Lowlands. One of the seemingly minor pieces of legislation introduced in 1784 to simplify the taxation laws was the introduction of what became known as the Highland Line, a somewhat arbitrary line running roughly along the Ochil hills from Glasgow to Dundee. Anything north of this line was regarded as Highland and taxed at a much lesser degree than in the Lowlands. Steadily increasing taxation on whisky from 1784, led to more and more illicit distilling in the Highlands where, unlike the Lowlands, it was still very much more a cottage industry practiced on every croft and small farm to make ends meet. Without the income from distilling whisky it would have been impossible for the average highland tenant farmer of this period to pay his rent.

The shape of the still

In the early days the stills varied very greatly in size and shape but by the end of the 18th century they had mostly standardised into something approaching the modern form, which evolved largely because of the need to distil at a great speed to beat the taxation system. Naturally enough the illicit stills were nothing like as elaborate as those which were legally taxed. By the late 18th century, however, there were several master coppersmiths openly advertising their wares in Inverness under the sign of a ater. whisky still.

An illicit still

A simple illicit still might be made from a cauldron with a cover and a spout fitted tightly in place with tow, like a lid. The spout would lead off to a coil, or worm, a spiral of copper tubing, often enclosed in a barrel with cold water from a nearby burn flowing through it to hasten the cooling process. With the cooling came the condensation of the spirit. Such primitive stills could be readily moved and were usually sited in a convenient cave, or hollow, on a hillside close to a burn supplying readily available water.

The distilling process

Sufficient sacks of barley would be steeped in the burn for around three days before being spread out to germinate in the cave, or a convenient barn. The germinating barley had to be turned every day for some ten days before being dried over a peat fire to halt the germination when it was felt to have reached the right stage. This malted barley was then placed in a mash tun, generally a large barrel, and water was poured over it. This was then stirred every few hours until the resulting mixture was drained off into another barrel and the process repeated. The liquor resulting from this process was and still is known as wort and the product of these two soakings of the grain would then be mixed together in a larger barrel and yeast would be added to them to assist in the fermentation. The resulting liquid, known as low wash, would then be heated and put through the still and became transformed into low wines. The still had then to be thoroughly cleaned before the low wines were put through it again, with the end result finally becoming malt whisky. This method, greatly refined and using two separate pot stills, is more or less how malt whisky is produced today.

The Act of 1823

In 1823 after a Board of Trade Commission had reported on the facts to Parliament a reforming Act to eliminate illegal distilling was introduced with the support of the Duke of Gordon. A flat rate of £10 was introduced on all stills of forty gallons upwards and a duty of 2s 3d placed on each gallon of spirits distilled. Encouraged by the Duke of Gordon, one of the first to take advantage of the new act was George Smith in Glenlivet, despite threats from his neighbours to burn down his distillery.

The effect of The Act of 1823

The immediate result was that within two years the amount of tax-paid whisky had increased from two million to six million gallons annually. The long term effect was to change what had amounted to little more than a cottage craft into a considerable industry which by the end of the century was to become one of Scotland's principal assets. The results of too high taxation on the industry are something that should still be borne in mind and it may be argued that this stage has already been reached and passed with as dire effects on the industry today as in 1820. (In 1995 when tax returns from Scotch Whisky fell by £35 million Chancellor Kenneth Clarke was promptly forced to reduce the tax increase he had just introduced and repeat a further similar tax reduction in 1996. This did not stop Chancellor Gordon Brown in 1997 reverting to tax increases, but the warning signals are set at red and clear to see.)

Pot-still distilling: first stage

The method of producing malt whisky by pot still distillation was by this time well developed. The best available Scottish barley as transported to the distillery by pack-horse, cart or boats, where it was placed in large steeps, or tanks. Water was then poured over and it was left for around 48 hours to soak thoroughly. It was then spread on the floor of the malting shed with its characteristic Chinese pagoda-like roof ventilators and was left for something like eight days to reach the right stage of germination. To regulate the degree of heat in the malting barley it was turned at regular intervals. When the required state of germination had been reached the starch in the barley had all by this time been transformed into sugar. It was then heated in a kiln over peat fires to check the germination thus imparting a peaty smokey flavour to the whisky.

Second stage

The malted grain was then bruised in the mill before being put into the mash tun where heated water was added and the mixture stirred. The peaty water would add its own flavour and with added yeast the mixture, now known as wort, fermented in special fermenting vats for some three days during which the sugar was converted into alcohol. The resulting wash was then led into the wash still, standing beside the spirit still.

The wash still and the spirit still

In any malt whisky distillery today the wash still and spirit still may be seen standing side by side, at first sight apparently identical to each other. The wash in the wash still is heated to boiling point when the alcohol rises through the worm, or coil, in its cold water jacket. It is then discharged as low wines directly into the adjacent spirit still. The same process of heating the low wines to boiling point then takes place and the same process ensues but this time the spirit produced is malt whisky. This in turn is then placed in oak casks, preferably casks in which sherry had been kept, and is aged for a minimum of three, but generally nearer eight to ten years, or sometimes as much as twelve, fifteen or more, before becoming accepted as the finest drink that any country could produce.

Unique to Scotland

The process of malt whisky pot-still distillation today is in essentials virtually unchanged from the first quarter of the 19th century. The whiskies themselves, even when produced in almost identical areas, using apparently identical pot stills and even when using the same water supply are never the same. Despite all efforts to duplicate the process in other countries the distilling of Scotch malt whisky remains unique to Scotland.

The silent season

During the summer months, when the burns and springs supplying the old distilleries tended to run dry, and when it often grew too warm for the malting process to be carried through successfully, distilling was abandoned for several weeks during what was termed the 'silent season'. During this period distillery maintenance and repairs were usually carried out. As the autumn set in distilling would then start again. Some distilleries even today have a silent season when repairs are carried out and distilling is discontinued.

The introduction of the continuous patent-still

In 1828 a new invention revolutionised the whisky industry when Robert Stein, one of the Lowland whisky distilling family, produced the first continuous patent still. This distilled in one continuous process, without the double distillation required in pot-still distillation. Only four years later in 1832 Aeneas Coffey, an ex-Inspector General of Excise in Ireland, patented a simpler continuous still which became known as the Coffey still and quickly superseded Stein's more cumbersome invention.

The patent-still

The continuous still is basically little more than two 40 feet high copper columns side by side, linked by a junction pipe at the top. These are known as the analyser and rectifier and each column consists of a number of horizontal compartments containing perforated copper plates. A jet of steam is passed through these columns and the wash is pumped into the still through a pipe coiled around the length of the rectifier from the top downwards, both cooling the latter and also heating the wash before it enters the top of the analyser column. On entering the analyser column the heated wash encounters an upwards pressure of steam surging through the perforated chambers. Since alcohol boils and evaporates at lower temperatures than water the alcohol separates from the wash as it descends chamber by chamber through the perforated plates. The alcohol then rises with the steam and entering the base of the rectifier column condenses on the perforated plates of each chamber. The purest alcohol rises to the top and the heavier higher alcohols and lower alcohols condense at lower levels since they have lower boiling points and are drawn off for re-distilling. The end product of this method of distilling is almost pure alcohol and since it is a continuous process can be continued as long as wash is available to put through the still.

Grain Whisky

The whisky produced by this process became known as patent-still, or grain, whisky, to differentiate it from the malt whisky produced by the malt whisky distillers, using the slower traditional method requiring two pot stills. The grain whisky distillers were naturally able to produce far greater quantities of their whisky than the malt whisky distillers and there was keen rivalry between the two, with the slower pot-still distillers inevitably the losers. Since almost all the new patent stills were situated convenient to the large centres of population in the Lowlands there was also an element of the familiar antagonism between Highlander and Lowlander which is even today to be found not far below the surface.

The merchants

The middle-men who sold the whisky in the mid-19th century, many of whom at this stage were little more than family grocers, began to grow in importance with the growth of the Scotch whisky industry itself. Like middle-men in many other industries they reaped considerable profits and their power developed to the stage where they could dictate their own terms to the whisky distillers, more especially the small pot-still malt whisky producers. Being individualists to a man the latter especially were very slow to combine and

11

while the rest of the Scotch whisky industry gradually began to merge and consolidate they were the last to see the advantages of union.

Whisky at this stage

The patent-still, or grain, whisky was made from any grain, oats, rye, or maize, crushed and boiled to break up the starch. During the mashing process a little malted barley would be added then fermentation on a large scale would take place. The result was that it was not only produced in much larger quantities, but it was much quicker, cheaper and easier to produce than the slow twice distilled, pot-still distillation methods. Furthermore it was generally much more even, being more or less tasteless pure spirit. The malt distillers, seldom operating with more than two or four stills and relying largely on the skill of the individual still-man supervising the distilling process, often produced very varying single malt whiskies, (i.e. malt whisky from one distillery unmixed with any other) which not only tasted very strong to southern palates, but also varied considerably with each distilling. To the discerning the differences might be both interesting and desirable, but they did not make it easy to sell. It was only when grain whisky was added to single malt whiskies to make a standardised blend that was smoother and more acceptable to southern palates that sales began to rise.

Blended Whisky

From the 1850s onwards, especially, the growth of the Scotch whisky industry was dramatic. It was a merchant, Andrew Usher & Co., agent for The Glenlivet malt whisky who is credited with first introducing blended whisky in 1853. The term blended whisky, was at first used to describe a mixture of malt whiskies, now known as vatted malts, but in time came to be used as today to describe the addition of malt whisky to grain whisky, making the blended Scotch whiskies we know today. At the time it is doubtful if the full significance of this innovation was appreciated, but inevitably it led to cut-throat competition in the industry as the trade expanded over the second half of the 19th century. By that time, however, the industry had shed its old illicit image and was highly organised with a Customs man then present in each distillery who had charge of a set of keys providing sole access to the Spirit still and bonded store where the whisky produced was kept to mature.

The early cartels

The earliest 'trade arrangement', as it was euphemistically termed, was entered into in 1856 by six firms of distillers. In the 1860s the cartel was re-formed and in 1877 the firms concerned decided to merge. They were: John Bald & Co., Carsebridge Distillery, Alloa; John Haig & Co., Cameron Bridge Distillery, Fife; Macfarlane & Co., Port Dundas Distillery, Glasgow; MacNab Bros & Co., Glenochil Distillery, Menstrie; Robert Mowbray, Cambus Distillery, Alloa; Stewart & Co., Kirkliston Distillery, Lothian. Together they formed The Distillers Company Limited, based in Edinburgh, which steadily developed by merger and take-overs to become the leading force in the industry for the best part of a hundred years, attaining its greatest period of strength before and after the 1939-45 War.

The brand names

From around 1853 to the 1870s the blended whiskies sold in the south were often little more than grain whisky with a minimal amount of malt, pot-still, whisky added. Nevertheless a number of very able reputable merchants and distillers began to emerge producing recognised standard whiskies with specific brand names. With consummate salesmanship they spread the sales of Scotch not only throughout England but onto the continent and throughout the British Empire and elsewhere in the civilised world. As a result of their efforts blended whisky came to be recognised throughout the world as the product of Scotland.

Phylloxera vastatrix and 'The Big Five'

The effect of *Phylloxera vastatrix*, a lethal insect which attacked the roots of the vines, on the French wine and, hence also the brandy, producers had been disastrous in the 1870s and '80s and the producers of Scotch whisky were not long in seizing their opportunity. Scotch whisky soon came to fill the gap in the market. Famous names such as James Buchanan's 'Black and White', Peter Mackie's 'White Horse', Alexander Walker's 'Johnnie Walker', The Dewar brothers, John and Tommy, John Haig and others had begun to dominate the industry. These, however, were widely known as 'The Big Five', who were all recognised and celebrated salesmen and founders of famous brand names of various blended whiskies sold widely throughout the world and also widely advertised. The flamboyant salesmanship of Tommy Dewar endeared him to the Press and the public, even if it was his brother John who was the steadying influence. James Buchanan's tall handsome figure and considerable presence made him a powerful personality in any company. Peter Mackie too was a man who naturally hit the headlines and influenced the industry. These were amongst the men who dominated the whisky industry during the boom years of the 1880's and 90's. Although the Distillers Company Limited was the growing power behind the scenes, which ultimately under the superb direction of William Ross was to take them all over, they were the names the public chiefly associated with the Scotch whisky industry at this time and to a large extent they were also responsible for its rapid growth.

Malt Whisky distillers

This is not to say that the pot-still malt whisky distillers were unable to survive. There were still many small malt whisky distillers and despite the strong and powerful Lowland grain distillers and the power of the merchants they managed to keep going for there were still considerable local sales within Scotland itself, as well as regular sales to discriminating merchants and blenders who knew what they required. At this stage there were several clear groupings of pot-still malt whisky distillers. There were basically the Highland distillers, notably in Speyside based mainly round the Central Highland Speyside area, and the Lowland distillers below the Highland Line to be found as far south as Dumfriesshire and East Lothian. There were also those on the

Islands, mainly on the west coast, particularly on Islay. There were in addition 34 concentrated in and around the west coast town of Campbeltown, then known as the malt whisky capital of Scotland. Most of these area groupings, with the notable exception of Campbeltown, remain in existence today.

The end of the Scotch Whisky boom

Although by the 1890s most of the big brand names we know today such as 'Black & White', 'Haig', 'Queen Anne', 'Johnnie Walker' and 'Vat 69' to name only a few, were selling well throughout the world there were also many dubious fly-by-night firms cashing in on the boom by selling whisky of a very low standard at inflated prices. One of the more flamboyant and dubious firms blending and selling their own whisky at this time were Pattison's Ltd, controlled by two brothers, Robert and Walter Pattison, who had started as dairy wholesalers and graduated to dispensing whisky because they felt there was more profit in that than in selling watered milk. They found they could buy cheap grain whisky at under 1s (5p) a gallon and by adding a minute quantity of malt whisky could sell it at 8s 6d (42½p)a gallon, describing it as 'Finest Glenlivet'. One of their more bizarre attempts at advertising included distributing to their retailers some 500 parrots which were allegedly trained to say 'Drink Pattison's Whisky'. Despite, or because of, such sales methods they went bankrupt in 1898 to the then almost unheard of sum of £82,000. Investigation soon revealed fraud on a large scale as well as making public the more deplorable methods of blending used by the disreputable end of the whisky industry. Their trial, combined with the outbreak of the Boer War, brought the whisky boom to an abrupt end. It also brought before the public attention for the first time the argument of the pot-still whisky distillers that grain whisky was not really Scotch whisky.

The Islington Borough Council

In 1906 the Islington Borough Council took a local publican to court for selling grain whisky alleging that this was 'not of the nature, substance and quality demanded by the purchaser.' The Distillers Company Limited failed to take the case seriously and the result seemed a resounding triumph for the pot-still malt distillers when it was held that 'whisky should consist of a spirit distilled in a pot-still derived from malted barley' . . .'

The Royal Commission of 1909

Although at first hailing this legal decision as a resounding victory, the malt whisky distillers quickly realised that the enormously wealthy Lowland distillers would simply distil very cheap Lowland malts and use them instead of their Highland malts to produce blended whisky. Both sides therefore asked for a Royal Commission to decide the issue and after eighteen months, in 1909, the Commission very sensibly concluded that' whiskey (the current spelling of the period) is a spirit obtained by the distillation of a mash of cereal grains saccharified by the diastase of the malt; that 'Scotch whiskey' is whiskey, as above defined, distilled in Scotland . . .' This definition of Scotch whisky was finally incorporated in Statute Law (as late as 1952) and is thus accepted by every government throughout the world. Because of this ruling Scotch whisky may not be distilled in any other country in the world.

Increasing taxation

The first increase in taxation for forty years took place in 1900 when it was raised to 11s (55p) from the 10s (50p) per gallon set by Gladstone in 1860. In 1909, taking full advantage of the split in the industry resulting from the Royal Commission's findings David Lloyd George, then Chancellor of the Exchequer and a lifelong rabid teetotaller, raised the tax per proof gallon by a further 3s 9d (18½p) to 14s 9d (73½p). Without united opposition from within the industry the increase was passed, a foretaste of things to come and a warning to both distillers and merchants of the dangers of lacking unanimity.

The Scottish Malt Distillers Limited

Just before the outbreak of the 1914-18 War the Distillers Company Limited, already the most powerful moving force in the industry, amalgamated five Lowland Malt Whisky distillers into a group called the Scottish Malt Distillers Limited. Inevitably many of the malt whisky distilleries which found themselves unable to survive the rigours of the war years were absorbed into this growing DCL subsidiary.

The effects of the 1914–18 War

The DCL was large enough to survive the war years and even prosper under the able directorship of its outstanding managing director, William Ross. Its patent still distilleries were employed in producing industrial alcohol for wartime use. During the entire war the DCL continued to expand, through mergers, amalgamations and take-overs. In 1917 the government restricted distilling solely to producing industrial alcohol. The Central Liquor Control Board also decreed that all spirits should be diluted to 50 under proof or 70% proof. The industry responded by forming the Whisky Association, a central body to defend the interests of all distillers, both patent-still and pot-still, blenders, merchants and exporters. In spite of this the price of whisky rose from 20s to 80s owing to lack of controls.

From 1918–20

In 1918 seeking a means of financing the enormous costs of the war the government more than doubled the tax per proof gallon of whisky from 14s 9d (73½p) to 30s (£1.50), a total rise of 15s 5d. This naturally produced more revenue in the short term and encouraged the Chancellor of the Exchequer to add a further 20s (£1) in 1919 making the total tax a matter of 50s (£2.50) per proof gallon, more than trebling the level of taxation within three years. In 1920 the government went even further and raised the tax by 22s 6d (£1.12½) to 72s 6d (£3.62½)per proof gallon, thus making a fivefold increase within three years, the sort of burden which would inevitably be a strain on any industry, not least one attempting to recover from the effects of a major war.

Prohibition

The year 1920 also saw the introduction of Prohibition in the United States of America. Pot-still malt distilling had only been permitted to start again in 1919 with the distillers looking forward to a minor boom in post-war years. The effects of the high taxation and Prohibition caused a major depression in the industry instead and this lasted throughout the 1920s until the end of Prohibition in 1932, by which time that imprudent if well intentioned experiment had been totally discredited. During this period of depression in the industry only the DCL empire was sufficiently strong and powerful to continue to expand. Four of the 'Big Five', Haig, Johnny Walker, Buchanan and Dewar, had already been amalgamated, and finally in 1927, but only after his death, Sir Peter Mackie's White Horse Distillers, were also absorbed into the DCL. The DCL was by then the only company in the whole industry sufficiently powerful to continue to open up new fields abroad, but even so it was mainly by diversification that it survived successfully, especially after the Great Depression of 1930.

The Pot-Still Malt Distillers Association

In 1926 the Pot-Still Malt Distillers Association of Scotland was formed to replace the old North of Scotland Malt Distillers Association as an all-embracing association of all Scottish Malt Whisky distillers. It is, however, indicative of how deeply the Depression had affected the industry that in 1933 the Association recommended to its members that there should be no distilling at all that year and by that time there were only fifteen distilleries operating in the whole of Scotland with several of these only operating on a part-time basis. Although the DCL then controlled 33 Highland distilleries in addition to five in Campbeltown and five in Islay most of these had merely been acquired in order to close them down. Excessive taxation and the closure of the major market of the USA had brought the industry close to total ruin.

The 1930s

From the repeal of Prohibition in 1930 to the outbreak of War in 1939 the industry began to recover. The process started gradually but speeded up as the world markets began slowly to expand. The outbreak of war was not entirely unexpected but was naturally a grave blow, as was the imposition of a further 10s (50p) tax per proof gallon in 1939 raising it to 82s 6d (£4.12½).

The 1939–45 War

In 1940 the duty per proof gallon was raised by 15s (75p) to 97s 6d (£4.87½) and distilling was restricted. It was then prohibited altogether from 1941–45. This did not prevent the tax being raised again in 1942 by a further 40s (£2) to 137s 6d (£6.87½) and yet once more in 1943 by a further 20s (£1) to 157s 6d (£7.87½). From 1945 onwards distilling on a small scale was permitted for pot-still malt whisky distillers only, to earn much-needed dollar currency.

The Scotch Whisky Association

In 1942, recalling their experiences after the 1914-18 War and to provide the industry with the maximum security possible, the Whisky Association was wound up and replaced by the Scotch Whisky Association. Its primary objectives are: to protect and promote the interest of the Scotch whisky trade generally both at home and abroad and to do all things and take all such measures as may be conducive or incidental to the attainment of such objects.

1945–50

Although only very limited, pot-still malt distilling had been permitted from 1944 onwards to earn much needed dollar currency this did not stop Hugh Dalton, Chancellor of the Exchequer in 1947 raising the tax per proof gallon by 33s 4d

(£1.66½) to 190s 10d (£9.54). In 1948 his successor Sir Stafford Cripps added a further 20s (£1) to the tax making it £10 10s 10d (£10.54) per proof gallon. At the same time only licenses to distil for export were granted, yet inevitably every increase of taxation in Britain was followed by corresponding increases in taxation abroad. It might be said the government cut the throat of their goose while it laid its golden eggs and that many of the ills affecting the industry may be traced back to this period.

The 1950s

Throughout the 1950s the Scotch whisky industry, already greatly weakened by the war years and by excessive taxation, was faced with fresh competition, much of it from North America, in part at least financed by British Government subsidies. It could be claimed this was not only cutting the golden goose's throat, but chopping off its limbs and feeding them to the fox for a short-term financial return.

The 1960s

In spite of repeated warnings of the inevitable effects on the industry, throughout the 1960s successive governments continued the negative policy of raising the tax per proof gallon almost annually. The tax was increased in 1961, 1964, 1965, 1966 and 1968, by which time it had reached £18.85 pence per proof gallon. The industry sought to protect itself by amalgamations and forming ever larger groups.

The 1970s

During the 1970s, although a similar process continued, there were different forces at work. The British currency was decimalised in 1971. In 1973 with the introduction of Value Added Tax and the entry of Britain into the European Economic Community the duty on whisky was actually reduced for the first time since 1896. This did not deter successive governments from raising the tax per proof gallon every year from 1973 to 1977. By then the tax per proof gallon amounted to £27.09. This represented duty on a bottle of whisky at the rate of £3.16. Further mergers, amalgamations and take-overs resulted during this period.

The 1980s

This steady investment of foreign capital into what had always been an intensely Scottish industry continued throughout the 1980s. This was a period of severe recession, but the damage had been done, nor did the process halt. Investment from Japan, the Far East, Europe, Canada and North America continued, taking full advantage of government subsidies. Once established such companies did not always act with the genuine long-term, or even sometimes short-term, interests of the Scotch whisky industry - or for that matter of Scotland, or indeed Britain - at heart. Little else could be expected. To encourage foreign investment to set up in competition and even subsidising them to do so could hardly be desirable and clearly proved in some cases against the best interests of the industry and of the country. For instance, bulk export of Scotch whisky, especially immature stocks, by such firms, undoubtedly damaged the industry's standing and prestige abroad. This was particularly difficult to control and is merely one of the ways in which the industry has been and may continue to be adversely affected. Along with excessive taxation this absence of overall control emphasised the lack of understanding of successive governments based in London. Control of a large part of the industry was also transferred to London following the 1987 disputed acquisition by Guinness of DCL, later merged with Arthur Bell & Sons and re-named United Distillers plc, and other parts are controlled from North America, Europe and Japan. The result was a serious financial loss to Scotland and a disastrous situation created by successive governments. By the end of the 1980's the position began to resemble a distorting mirror image of the period prior to 1824 when government actions had brought about a crisis in the industry and it seemed that matters could be satisfactorily resolved only by radical action such as was taken then.

The International Organisation of Legal Metrology

Since 1980 Britain has adopted the standard system of proof measurement of the Common Market, measuring alcohol by percentage of volume at 20° C. Sikes 70° equals IOLM 39.9% and 75° = 42.8%: 80°=45.6%: 100° = 57.1%: 120° = 68.5%: Malt whisky may be purchased at 70°–105° proof measured by Sikes's method. This means they vary from approximately 40% to 60% volume. A proof gallon contains 57.1% alcohol by volume and is 100% proof. 1 gallon = 4.546 litres = 180 fl.'oz. 1 gallon = 6 bottles of 26⅔fl.oz = 75 centilitres or 4 bottles of 40 fl. oz. A proof litre = 100% alcohol by volume and the standard bottle contains 70cl.

The 1990s

As part of the European Economic Community it was decreed that Scotch whisky should be recognised as Scotch whisky only if it is distilled and produced in Scotland. Furthermore it must be no less that 40% volume, since at anything less it cannot be checked that it is indeed Scotch whisky. Throughout the decade continued foreign owner-ship and financial stringency, too often resulted in standards slipping, especially when control passed into the hands of accountants based overseas interested chiefly in the quickest possible returns on their investments. That is a recipe for disaster which has resulted in bankruptcies in other largely foreign controlled industries in Scotland and the UK. Parts of the industry were also too often seduced, as they had been during the previous decade or more, by these twin PR weasel-words, marketing and presentation, into change sim-ply for the sake of change, whether it is new bottles, new labels, new colouring or new advertising. New and larger groupings have not always proved beneficial either to the investment corporations or to the distilleries involved. The successions of take-overs and mergers involving enormous financial corporations almost totally unconnected with whis-ky industry, a trend which has been noticeable since the 1939 War, but sharply accentuated in the nineties, has been followed in almost every case by accountancy 'rationalisa-tions,' frequently involving distilleries closing or changing hands. This can only destabilise an industry that depends for much of its success on continuity and long-term planning, not only in finance but also in manpower and commitment. Successive governments have also contributed to this trend by their constant use of the industry as a milch cow for excessive taxation. A public acknowledgement of the damage being caused to the industry by excessive taxation came at last in 1995 when a slump of £36 million in revenue returns forced Chancellor Kenneth Clarke to cancel his tax rise for that year and in 1996 to make the first considerable reduction in tax since 1824, although this did not deter his successor Chancellor Douglas Brown from raising it again in 1997.

Scottish Distilleries

Another bright feature of the decade has been the emergence of several new small distilleries aiming towards individual excellence once again in an industry too often now dominated by larger financial combines. Size does not necessarily promote greater excellence especially in an industry noted for the individuality and character both of its' products and its' producers. There are, fortunately, still some entirely Scottish based and Scottish owned distilleries and groups making their individual contributions and more than holding their own in this quintessentially Scottish industry. Long may that continue. A classic example of the converse has been the disappearance of the name Whyte & Mackay, first a subsidiary of Gallaghers USA, then of American Brands Inc, and latterly of Jim Beam Brands (Worldwide) Inc., now using as its' European subsidary the name Jim Beam Brands (Greater Europe) plc. As part of a rationalisation plan, imposed presumably by a bunch of gin-swilling New York accountants, the name of the firm owning the distilleries at the Scottish end has latterly been changed from Whyte & Mackay to the name of Jim Beam Brands, owners of Jim Beam bourbon whiskey, used in abbreviated form as JBB (Greater Europe) plc. That many Scots may not consider themselves part of Europe, that bourbon has no place in Scotch whisky beyond some of the casks used for maturation and that this may be seen as the same sort of ignorant arrogance displayed by Hollywood when Errol Flynn was depicted winning the 1945 war is something they obviously do not appreciate. What may seem a convenient rationalisation in New York is not necessarily a good sales gimmick for selling Scotch whisky in Scotland or indeed anywhere outside the USA.

From the year 2000 onwards into the future

Now that Scotland has a Parliament of its' own it is time, at last, to take steps to control its foremost industry, since the Scotch Whisky Association, although a very effective trade association, has no mandate beyond those agreed by its' members amongst themselves. By introducing a greater degree of control and passing those powers to a freshly created government-backed body with the interests of the industry and of Scotland at heart the situation could be greatly improved. As a first step, for instance, each firm or corporation controlling two or more malt whisky distilleries might by law be forced to base a corporate management headquarters in Scotland. This is an industry where time-tried methods and generations of experience are all-important assets too frequently ignored. Large scale marketing methods and constant attempts to introduce new sales strategies and gimmicks, new bottles, new labels, new flavours and new colourings to name only a few examples of frequently used sales strategies and techniques are often in the end self-defeating as the past decades have shown. One of the first attempts to demonstrate the individuality of malt whiskies was DCL's, now UDV's, packaging in 1988 of its 'Classic Malts' series, of six individual malt whiskies differing largely because of their geographical situation. i.e. Lowland, Islay, Highland, Speyside.

More than Geographical Differences

There is, of course, far more to malt whisky than geographical differences and it should be a matter for congratulation and indeed a good selling point that there may be differences in each separate distilling of a malt whisky and in each cask and for that matter that some malt whiskies mature much faster than others, while there are also some very slow to mature. In 1995 DCL, now UDV, appreciated this and introduced an extensive Rare Malt selection, bottling single malts from individual casks often of considerable age and differing strengths, sometimes from distilleries long-closed. They followed this by introducing 'Distillers Editions' of some of their single malts, giving the year it was distilled. Some distilleries were already ahead of them and by now many are offering selected bottlings of up to fifty years old at cask strength. Whether such inevitably costly bottles of malt whisky are seen as an investment or as a drink is almost by the way. These are considerable steps towards increasing the public interest in single malt whiskies as well as a shrewd attempt to secure a share of the market for special malt bottlings already created by Gordon & Mac-Phail, William Cadenhead, the Scotch Malt Whisky Society and other independent bottlers. This is also a move towards the lines I have long advocated of following the example set by the wine growing districts of France, labelling the product not only by date, but by some indication of the excellence attained in normal production, not just specially produced casks. The distillery's name on the label of a malt whisky thus becomes roughly equivalent to *Appelation Controle* and *premier cru* on a wine bottle, giving some indication of the standard to be expected beyond those at present customary. In due course, perhaps, some independent Scottish based body interested in promoting Scotch Whisky, such as the Keepers of the Quaich, might introduce annual awards for malt whiskies aged in the cask for specific periods, corresponding to *Grand Cru*, using the Gaelic adjective Mohr, meaning Great, thus creating *A Malt Whisky Mohr*. The aim should be individuality and variety in taste and excellence. That is what malt whisky is all about.

Highland
Lowland - and Island

A General Introduction to Scotch Whisky
and to
The Directory of Malt Distilleries

A Foreword on Scotch Whisky

It is important to understand something of the background of Scotch whisky and the industry as a whole before examining the pot-still malt whiskies more closely. In this brief introduction it is impossible to cover every aspect of the Scotch whisky industry in detail and only a general outline can be given. As noted above, for instance blending Scotch whisky is a skilled task which has been developed to a high degree over the years. It is accomplished by experts who 'nose' their various whiskies, savouring the bouquet and making up the various proportions which form the final blend. As many as thirty, or more, single malt whiskies may be used along with grain whisky to make up a specific blend. Year after year their task is to produce exactly the same taste in their blend. The major recognised blends do not alter very perceptibly in taste over the years entirely owing to their expertise. Knowing also the particular tastes of the countries to which their blends are destined for export they can subtly alter them to match the required demand, not only for taste but also for colour. It was the consistency of blended Scotch whisky in the 19th century, which made it easier to sell it to the general public, who knew what to expect when they bought a bottle. By contrast the pot still malt whiskies of the day frequently varied with each distillation so that they were often very different in taste. It was not until the malt distillers also turned to nosing their product and to quality control, producing a consistently recognisable standard brand, that they began to increase their market considerably. The age factor then also

27

entered the equation, since by law no mixture of whiskies may be sold as older than its youngest constituent.

Whisky and Nosing

Unlike wine it is not possible simply to taste whisky by swilling the neat spirit round the mouth. To do so would merely be to destroy the sense of taste almost immediately. A single measure of whisky should be poured into a tulip shaped glass, although a wine glass is satisfactory for most purposes, and at 40% volume a similar quantity of pure water added. If the aroma is then smelt the expert may deduce the origins of the blend or, if a malt, the details of its' distilling and maturing process, i.e. which distillery it came from and the type of cask in which it was matured. When the volume is greater he or she will require to add more pure water accordingly. He or she will also always start with the less powerful and go on to the stronger more highly flavoured, since to do otherwise would be to miss the more delicate scents. These of course, would be lost if chlorinated tap water was used instead of pure water. A heavy smoker, or someone addicted to peppermints or chewing gum, or strong tasting foods like curries, or anyone with a cold, is unlikely to be able to achieve much by nosing. It is essential to keep the sense of smell and taste as acute as possible, but given practice even a heavy smoker may appreciate something of the differences between malts in this way.

Whisky and Colour

The blender will also bear in mind the colour of whisky preferred by the customer. For instance the majority of States in the USA prefer a light coloured whisky, perhaps on the grounds that a large measure of light coloured whisky does not appear any darker in the glass than a small measure. In India a darker whisky is preferred. Since whisky when distilled is almost colourless some degree of colouring is therefore often added. Although malt whisky may acquire a certain amount of colour while it is being matured in old oak sherry casks it is an open secret that this can also be due to added caramel or even sherry. Blenders in practice will have a colour chart available to assist them and it is not a difficult matter to produce any colour that is required. Black whisky has been tried with little success. So far, thank goodness, no-one has tried to market pink whisky like pink champagne, but no doubt it will not be long before this too is tried.

The Supervision of the Pot-still Distillery

Ideally the distiller himself should supervise each aspect of the operation from buying the barley direct from the farmer to converting it into malt on the floor of the maltings, seeing that it is carefully turned with wooden rakes on the floor of the maltings and at the right moment dried over peat fires for the mashing and distilling processes. In modern distilleries most of these procedures are now largely automated and the malted barley itself will be obtained from an outside source, but there still has to be an experienced distillery manager in every distillery to oversee the entire operation and there are other important individuals in the employ of any pot-still malt distillery on whom a great deal depends. In some of the older established distilleries such skilled employees may sometimes be the second or even third generation of the same family

The Stills and the Still-man

There is no doubt that the actual shape of the stills affects the taste of the spirit produced. A long necked still tends to allow the heavier vapours rising through it to condense before reaching the swan neck and fall back into the heated distillate to be re-distilled thus generally producing a lighter, finer spirit. A short necked still by passing the heavier vapours through tends to produce a richer, fuller spirit. It is, however, the still-man, who is responsible for the actual distilling of the whisky. He it is who decides when to start distilling. On his judgement of when the foreshots have passed and when the 'middle cut' is running, much depends. Were he to start too soon or leave matters too late and allow the foreshots and after-shots to mix with the final spirit the result would not be up to standard. Much depends on him. Even in the best regulated of distilleries, however, it may sometimes happen that some foreshots or aftershots have crept into the distilling. Then it may be that a single bottle in a case has been filled with the last of a cask to the bottom of which the evil tasting oils have sunk. Although no distiller likes to admit it, such an unpleasant off-tasting bottle is sometimes found in any distillery's products, the equivalent of a corked bottle of wine, but it is a rare occurrence indeed.

The Master Cooper

The distillery should ideally also have a master cooper to supervise the casks in which the spirit is kept to mature. Whisky casks may often be used four or five times and thus may be of a considerable age, requiring regular careful checking and renewing. The wastage from such casks by evaporation can otherwise be considerable and add greatly to his costs. Some degree of evaporation in the cask, estimated at around 2% a year, is anyway inevitable and is known as 'the angel's share'. If the cooper or the still-man are not doing their jobs efficiently, however, the distillery can soon go to the wall and it is a fiercely competitive business.

The Casks

Until the early 20th century most whisky was sold by the distillers in whatever casks or barrels they had available. These were usually old wine or port casks but sometimes even old fish barrels were used which was said to be one of the reasons for the decline in popularity of whisky from Campbeltown, a major whisky distilling centre in the 19th century. The spirit was then bottled by the merchants, or sold by the publicans by the dram from stone or glass jars. In 1916 the government made it compulsory for whisky to be aged for a minimum of three years at least in the cask. In practice the casks are now always made of oak, which allows the spirit to breath. New casks were usually charred on the inside to remove the volatile woody elements present, hence why used casks were preferred. As they were obtainable at minimal cost many distillers favoured the oak casks in which sherry had been imported from Spain, but oak casks, which by US law may not be re-used for bourbon were also available very cheaply. Both types were commonly bought and usually taken apart and re-built by master coopers. Sherry butts contained 108 gallons (491 litres, roughly equivalent to 500 bottles at 40% volume after about 10 years) and whisky hogsheads 55 gallons (250 litres). Although sometimes used unaltered, the bourbon casks being slightly smaller than Imperial measure were usually rebuilt, five US casks making up four hogsheads. Then in the 1980s the Spanish government permitted bottling prior to export with a consequent rise in the cost of sherry casks. As long ago as 1890 the practice of soaking new wooden casks with cheap dark sherry before using them was introduced. Sometimes a compound called pajarate, a sweet colouring mixture made from grape juice and used in Jerez for sherries, was diluted and swilled round new casks to colour the wood before using them for whisky. Too much sherry in the whisky can lead to undue sweetness, or darker colouring, or even undesirable overtones in the whisky, masking the delicate flavours. Too much wood, which has not previously been used for maturing sherry, or spirit, may lead to an undesirably woody taste in the whisky stored in them. Too long in the cask may also lead to either of these undesirable results.

Varying the Cask

Even in the 19th century and certainly from quite early in the 20th century distillers were aware of the difference in taste produced by ageing in the cask and probably most had their preferences as to the type of casks used. Since the 1970s and '80's, however, many distillers have gone to considerable lengths and care in choosing their casks. Some have had their casks made in Spain and then used first for sherry before use. Some have even incurred substantial expenditure to ensure continuity in the type of oak used. Others have experimented with changing the type of cask during the process of ageing. For instance a whisky might spend some years in a sherry cask before being changed over to bourbon casks, or vice versa. Some distillers have experimented with casks that have held port, madeira or even rum or brandy. While some of these experiments are successful, there is always a danger of achieving undesirable overtones in a perfectly good whisky. Too strong a flavour of port, sherry, madeira, rum or anything else in a whisky can be distinctly unpleasant. This is a marketing gimmick that can easily be overdone, effectively ruining an otherwise excellent whisky. If anyone seriously wants a strong flavour of sherry, port, or madeira in their whisky they can always add it themselves.

Factors Affecting Flavour and Taste and Maturation

It is estimated that 60% of the final aromas and flavours in the whisky arise from the cask and the time spent in it. The remaining 40% it is claimed is due to the water, the barley and the production techniques, the shape and size of the stills and heating methods employed, also the micro-climate around the distillery, including the warehouse in which the casks are stored. It is, however. probably these latter factors which most directly affect whether a particular distillery produces a very fast or slow maturing malt whisky. Traditionally whisky warehouses are long and low with thick stone walls open windows and earth floors retaining the humidity and hence much less subject to temperature changes and subsequent loss due to evaporation. More modern solid floored warehouses are much drier, with casks stacked higher and, with temperatures more extreme at roof level, evaporation is likely to be greater. In Islay especially, where some warehouses are almost on the edge of the sea and subject to the extremes of Atlantic storms and sea spray, the effect is held to be considerable. Another factor affecting flavour and taste may take place during bottling when malt whisky is usually chill filtered, i.e. reduced in temperature to around freezing to remove certain fats that may cause the spirit to cloud when water is added, but which also contribute to the taste of the whisky Ultimately, however, taste is a matter for the individual and what is nectar to one man may taste like poison to another.

Ageing and maturing

By the legal definition of Scotch whisky contained in the Scotch Whisky Act 1988, no Scotch whisky may be sold under three years old and most are in fact kept in the cask until matured for five years at least. There is usually a particular age at which it is considered that most individual malt whiskies achieve their best. This may vary from five to eight years, for fast maturing malt whiskies, and on to ten or twelve, or even fifteen and upwards for more slowly maturing malt whiskies although in some cases more may be lost than gained after fifteen or so years. Two or three years then may often make an amazing difference. Some malt whiskies mature much faster than others and may be very drinkable after a mere three or four years when another neighbouring malt whisky may still taste very young and fiery. The same malt whisky may then be even better after a lapse of several years but sometimes in the intervening years goes through a period of further maturing when it may seem less desirable. This is one of the fascinating aspects of malt whisky as is the fact that each distilling is likely to be different from the last even if only very slightly. A longer term element to take into account is that as the individuals in charge of a distillery change over the decades so each malt whisky too can alter subtly in character, just as it may alter over the years in the cask. Taking into account other outside factors as well, such as temporary closures, mothballing, or take-overs of firms and it can be seen that over a thirty or forty year period for a variety of reasons the character of a malt whisky produced by a distillery may change radically. Where no age is given for a malt whisky it is reasonable to assume around five or at most six. Lowland malt whiskies are generally said to be mature enough to bottle at five years. It should be added that while whisky matures and alters perceptibly while kept in a cask it is unlike wine in that it does not alter materially once bottled.

Volume and Strength

It is a mistake to imagine that once distilled whisky is pure spirit. In fact the alcohol in whisky after distilling when measured by volume is usually only about 70%, although slightly more when triple distilled. With rare selected exceptions it is customary to add water to the whisky cask to reduce the contents to around a standard of 63.4% volume. During the bottling it is also standard practice to add more water to decrease the volume further to the standard European strength of 40% by volume or 43% for export. The distiller may decide to bottle some exceptional casks at a higher volume and occasional casks may even be bottled at 'cask strength,' i.e. without any further water being added. Depending on the age and size of the cask and the amount of evaporation, there may be only some hundred and fifty to two hundred and fifty bottles in a cask so that to be economic the price per bottle of such a malt whisky will have to be high.

Bottling

Very few malt whiskies are bottled by the distilleries themselves, although Glenfidich and Springbank are notable exceptions in this respect. The leading malt whiskies are usually bottled at bottling centres by the distillery owners in quantity in long runs to maintain an even quality control. Shorter runs and single casks are sometimes bottled by the distillers, (as for instance UDV's Rare Malts and Distiller's Edition of the 'Classic Malts') but are more usually bottled by or for the independent bottlers and merchants. or societies, such as the Scotch Malt Whisky Society. They may, or may not, be allowed to name the distillery from which it came since it is unlikely to taste at all like the usual product of the distillery, which has been nosed, quality controlled, chill filtered and prepared for sale to the public to meet a set standard.

Modern Technology

Sadly with the advent of larger and ever more automated systems of distilling even pot-still distilling is losing the individual touch in many places. The still-man may be seen controlling the whole business in a white coat and watching the dials on a computer. Where there are a number of stills in one distillery the likelihood is that the product of each spirit still will be mixed together to make up one standardised single malt whisky rather than allow the individual variations of each distilling to go through to the customer, which at one time made pot-still malt whiskies distinctive in the same way that each annual crop of the vineyards produces different vintages. With the advent of standardised blended whisky in the late 19th century, however, it was inevitable that eventually the pot-still malt distillers would have to follow suit. Today only two distillers malt their own barley (Springbank and Balvenie and the latter only about 10% of the total used.) The malted barley is obtained direct from the maltings and then processed through the mill and the mash tun ready for the wash still. It then goes through the wash still and the spirit still before reaching the casks. It is next stored in the warehouse in bond, i.e without duty payable. After it has matured for the time required, the casks will be nosed and as many casks as is considered necessary will be drained into a container, mixed, or vatted, together, and will eventually be bottled after a process which is likely to include chill filtering, testing for colour and general standardisation to produce an even end product which is easily recognisable by the customer as what he has come to expect. Although the marketing-men may argue speciously that quality control is all-important and that the customer likes to know in advance exactly what he is buying, preferring to buy a standard product each time, this may to some extent be mistaken reasoning. It could be a big mistake to think that the modern craving for standardisation should always be applied to malt whiskies.

The conglomerates

When the big conglomerates take over and try to streamline the industry with multiple stills, vast whisky vats and control by computer, something inevitably goes out of the product. Nor can it be good for any industry to have frequent closures and lay-offs resulting from large mergers and take-overs with the consequent loss of skilled workers and uncertainty as to the future. There are too many examples in other industries of foreign take-overs when large foreign conglomerates have taken over and tried to run what are essentially UK-based organisations from overseas with disastrous results. Sadly the foreign take-overs of pot-still malt distilleries and the big conglomerate acquisitions have gone almost unopposed because of successive governments' savage taxation of the whisky industry. Fortunately there are still some shining exceptions.

The Grants

The Grants, particularly, are a resilient clan, to which I am happy to be related, and they have had and continue to have a considerable influence on distilling in Scotland. It is a name which figures largely in any history of pot-still malt whisky distilling. There are of course many others also, who are concerned to see that pot-still distilling of Scotch malt whisky should continue in the traditional way to produce fine and distinctive single-malts. This part of the industry is fully alive and continuing to flourish with a significant part of it still under Scottish ownership and almost all under entirely Scottish management at least in Scotland. The emergence of a number of new small Scottish-owned malt distilleries in the past decade has also been an encouraging feature.

Grain Whisky and Blending

Fine Old Cameron Brig produced by Haig at their grain distillery at Glenrothes in Fife was for a long time notable as the only pure grain whisky for sale. The distillery has now been sold, but other grain whiskies are now available, notably Invergordon. By choosing your own malt whiskies and blending them with these it is, of course, possible to make your own blended whisky. It is also possible and pleasurable to mix your own malt whiskies to achieve perfection.

D.I.Y.

The beauty of Scotch whisky is that it is perfectly possible for discriminating drinkers to make up a blend, or a mixture of malt whiskies, known as a vatted malt whisky, entirely to their own taste, if they wish to find out whether they can improve on those produced commercially. There is little doubt that by choosing their blends shrewdly and adding a measure of malt whisky to them they can often greatly improve the blend they are drinking at least to their own satisfaction. The same is undoubtedly true of mixing malt whiskies and producing a vatted malt which is, to their particular taste, an improvement on the originals used to make up the end product. Contrasting malt whiskies by selecting three or four amongst the finest, then, after nosing and savouring them, taking a little of each in differing quantities together in one glass is always exciting. In this way nectar may be achieved, but in the nature of things it is a nectar that is constantly changing since the constituents themselves are seldom quite the same.

Changes in Character and Taste

Over the years, inevitably, malt whiskies slowly change and their characters alter as the men who make them and control their destiny also change. With changes in the ownership and management of distilleries, following take-overs and mergers, with temporary or longer closures resulting, such changes in the character of a malt whisky may be all too frequent. Even where the management of a distillery has remained unchanged for many years, however, it may be decided to market a spirit of a different age, strength and volume, or distilled from specially prepared malted barley, or matured in different casks, producing a malt whisky with an entirely different character and taste.

The Malt Whiskies

There are still over a hundred malt whisky distilleries to be found in Scotland. It is the malt whisky from these which provides the essential flavour of Scotch whisky, whether drunk individually, in conjunction with others as vatted malts, or as blended whisky mixed with grain, or patent-still, whisky. These malt whiskies are to the connoisseur what the *premier cru* wines are to the wine drinker. No two are alike and each separate bottling may differ from the last, although today a high degree of standardisation and quality control has been achieved. Whether this is always necessarily a good thing is another matter, but it has to be said that it does make the task of the blender easier. It is however still a matter for congratulation that even after being put through the modern process of quality control, each single malt whisky still has its own unique taste and aftermath.

The geography of Malt Whisky

The malt whiskies are widely separated geographically but there are basically only two main divisions, Highland and Lowland, from above and below the Highland Line. There are, however, quite a number of west coast Highland and northern Highland malt whiskies as well as a large grouping round Speyside. There are also Island malt whiskies, particularly the Islay group and those from Orkney. Fortunately the products of the different regions as well as of the individual distilleries remain each as different from the next as claret from burgundy or sherry from port. It is this that makes the malt whiskies so satisfying to savour even if there may be general similarities of type amongst the various groups. The large grouping around Speyside may have certain recognisable similarities, but they also differ widely from each other and from other Highland groups. The Islay malt whiskies also have their own very recognisable characteristics, but again differ very much from each other. The remaining Campbeltown malt whiskies still have a distinctive flavour of their own, as do the island malts of Arran, Jura and Mull (Tobermory) and those of Orkney, Highland Park and Scapa. So it is with the Lowland malt whiskies. There is a wealth of choice and interest for the enthusiast.

The Single Scotch Malt Whisky and Vatted Malts
A question of definition

If you wish to be exact it is correct to refer to the product of each pot-still malt whisky distillery in Scotland as a single

Scotch malt whisky. The reason for calling it Scotch malt whisky is that, although not many people are likely to encounter their products in this country, there is a pot-still malt whisky distillery in Ireland and three or four in Japan, notably Suntory's, started in 1923. The reason for terming it single is that even if what is in the bottle may be the result of several distillations it is the product of a single distillery as distinct from a vatted malt whisky which may be the product of several distilleries. This is, however, really being pedantic and leads to the absurdity that if you then wish to refer to the product of one distillation which has been casked as such, it has to be termed a 'single-single malt.' Vatting simply means mixing malt whiskies together. It is standard practice for a number of different casks of the same year of distilling from a single distillery to be mixed, or vatted, before bottling to produce a recognisable standard single malt whisky. A distillery may sometimes add an older cask to a younger single malt to add substance to it but it must then be sold at the age of the youngest. When, however, single malt whiskies from different distilleries are mixed, or vatted, they must then be sold as a Vatted Malt.

The labelling

The label on malt whisky bottles, like the shape of the bottles themselves, is liable to change from time to time, but there are certain points which should remain constant. It should specify that it is a product of Scotland, and that it is a pure malt whisky, giving the area from which it is produced and the name of the distillery and the name of the malt whisky itself, if different, as a few are. The alcoholic strength at which it is sold must be noted as must the quantity in the bottle. The age should also be given, although some malt whiskies are sold with the age unspecified. If it is bottled by an independent bottler this will be specified, in which case it must be appreciated that it cannot be regarded as a true sample of the distillery's product since such independent bottlings are liable to alter from year to year in strength and in age. To give the year of the bottling, as with a wine, means nothing unless the year in which is was distilled is also stated since whisky once in a bottle does not alter materially. If it is a blended whisky it should specify that it is Scotch whisky and a product of Scotland. It should also add, 'distilled, blended and bottled in Scotland.' If it is a vatted malt, probably styled *The Pride of this and that*, it may say that it is 'pure malt' and it may give an age, which, as is the case with blended or single malt whiskies, must be the age of the youngest constituent, but it will not include the name of a distillery. In some cases a single malt may be sold by a distillery in bulk to a major buyer, such as a Supermarket chain, on the understanding that it is not sold with the distillery's name on it. The buyer then sells it at a reduced price to their customers labelled as their 'special single malt,' probably named Glen this or that, but with only a general specification as to its' origins, i.e. Speyside, Islay, or Highland and without any specific distillery of origin. There should be no confusion and it is simply a question of reading the label of the bottle with care. The same applies to the very numerous blended whiskies which must of necessity be left outside the scope of this book, although a listing of some of the better known vatted malts has been included. (See pp. 185).

A question of taste

In describing taste, which is such an individual matter, it is next to impossible to be exact and what one man likes another may abhor. It may be said that every Scot is basically an east coast man or a west coast man, depending on which side of Scotland he was born. To the east coast man initially the west coast malts taste of seaweed and drains. To the west coast man the east coast malts taste of antiseptic. It is only by persevering that the east coast man will discover subtle differing flavours and the west coast man surprisingly delicate nuances of taste. I have tried to avoid generalities or vague descriptions such as nutty, which may be coconut or hazelnut or peanut or whatever, but describing what amounts to mere sensations is at times a near impossibility. There are various so-called 'tasting wheels' providing every sort of combination of flavours from lipstick and banana to denim and other unlikely possibilities, which strike me as more than a little far-fetched. Other poetic flights of fancy, suggesting for instance a peppermint or eau-de-cologne flavour to a whisky, are to my mind unhelpful and downright impossible, unless it is adulterated. As far as possible I have tried to indicate the taste as plainly as possible, but it is up to everyone to make up their own minds, that is half the pleasure of the drink.

A question of time and place

The short answer as to when it is best to drink Scotch whisky is any time you feel like it. In practice many outside factors must influence the matter. Extremes of temperature, whether of heat or cold, are one obvious factor. The state of mind and body are another. Clearly a dram is likely to be savoured with more appreciation after a day in the open air rather than in the smoky atmosphere of a city when no exercise has been taken. Scotch whisky can best be savoured in Scotland itself where it was distilled, but it travels well around the world and provides a taste of Scotland anywhere at any time. In the subsequent pages I have indicated that some malt whiskies may perhaps best be savoured before and some after a meal, but this is purely a pointer and in no sense a firm guide. Everyone should make their own decisions on when and where they wish to drink them.

How to drink Scotch Whisky

How anyone drinks Scotch whisky is entirely up to them. There are cocktails made from Scotch whisky, some of which are even drinkable. Some people prefer to drown the taste of their Scotch whisky in ginger ale, or orange juice. Others always insist on drinking their Scotch, whether malt or blend, neat, on the grounds that it is already watered before sale. Certainly some tap water tastes strongly of chlorine and other additives but to obtain the greatest satisfaction from a mature blend or a fine malt many people will rightly maintain that a little pure water improves the drink, probably as in 'nosing' at least an equal quantity of water at 40% volume, but remember even carbonated spring waters can alter the flavour of a fine malt whisky. What it is drunk from may also affect the taste. Fine glass, or crystal is probably preferable to plastic or china, and silver or metal cups may give it a metallic flavour, while a wooden quaich brings out the flavours to the full. It is, however, in the end a matter of individual choice and taste, for Scotch whisky in all its forms is a highly individual drink. It is the product of the country's lochs and rivers, of the barley, the peat, the labour and the centuries-old expertise of Scots. It is the very essence of Scotland itself. Drink it as you wish, but above all enjoy it

Independent bottling

There is nothing to stop anyone buying malt whisky in the cask and storing it, to have it bottled for themselves when they wish. In practice it is a very sensible way of buying malt whisky and various societies and syndicates with a special interest in malt whisky do so. Two independent bottlers in particular are also well known for the practice. These are Gordon & MacPhail Ltd, 58-60 South St, Elgin, Morayshire, IV30 1YJ and William Cadenhead Ltd, 172 Canongate, Edinburgh, EH8 8BN. Anyone interested in malt whisky owes a debt to these firms for providing many single malts which would otherwise be unobtainable. Indeed it is only through them that some bottles from long vanished distilleries are still available. The Scotch Malt Whisky Society, situated at The Vaults, Leith, 87 Giles St, Edinburgh, EH6 6BZ, performs a like service for some 16,000 members. There are half a dozen or so other whisky merchants who bottle independently. On the other hand since these bottlings vary considerably in age and strength it is unfair and unreasonable to attempt to relate them to a distillery's standard malt whisky. They are like an old, long bottled vintage port, delightful and rewarding, but by their very nature usually unrepeatable and not representative of modern standard bottlings. By introducing their range of Rare Malts and Special Editions of their 'Classic Malts,' UDV very shrewdly tapped into this steadily developing specialist market and now many distilleries have followed suit, offering whiskies of varying ages from thirty to fifty years and varying volume up to cask strength. Just as some people collect miniature bottles so some people collect rare whiskies. These may be expensive but may be seen as an investment like rare vintage wines, to be kept and not drunk. This to my mind defeats the whole object of both distilling and savouring malt whisky. Stick to stocks and shares for investing and whisky for drinking. Do not mix the two.

Publicity regarding distilleries and Scotch Whisky

Each distillery grouping is largely responsible for its own publicity, but there are certain bodies promoting the interests of Scotch Whisky that should be mentioned. The Scotch Whisky Association has already been noted as the Trade Association acting primarily within the industry and not as such concerned with publicity. 'The Keepers of the Quaich,' an organisation founded in 1987 by prominent members within the industry on the lines of a mediaeval Guild and now with world-wide connections, although not widely known to the general public, does a great deal to promote Scotch Whisky. For the average visitor to Scotland, however, The Scotch Whisky Heritage Centre, 358 Castlehill, Edinburgh, open seven days a week, (Tel: 0131 220 0441) by the Castle entrance, is fun and informative for visitors of any age and sex, from family parties to organised groups. Here you may learn painlessly all the facts about distilling and you can ride in half a whisky .cask for an audio-visual journey through the centuries giving all the information on Scotch Whisky anyone could want in six languages. Whisky tastings are also arranged. The Cairngorm Whisky Centre and Museum at Aviemore is also worth visiting, as is the old distillery at Dallas Dhu near Forres. (See p.161). The Scottish Tourist Board at Ravelston Crescent, Edinburgh (tel: 0131 332 2433) and local tourist offices in the Grampian and Highland Regions will also give details of those distilleries open for visitors, or on The Whisky Trail. Even where they have reception centres, however, their main task is still distilling whisky, so it is advisable to telephone beforehand.

Particulars of distilleries

To appreciate and savour malt whiskies to the full it is desirable to know something of each distillery itself and these are covered briefly in the pages which follow. It is important to know where each distillery is, a little of its background history, so that one can judge how much continuity and experience lies behind it, also who exactly owns it and to whom it is licensed, both very pertinent points. If you happen to be in the area it is as well to know whether you can visit it and whether it is accustomed to dealing with visitors. It is also important to know the age and strength when bottled of the standard distillery products. Finally, some idea of what the standard product tastes like cannot come amiss but here I have merely given some general guide lines with which the reader may or may not agree. In general where there are bottlings of exceptional age, type or specification by a distillery, such as UDV's Rare Malts, or cask strength products, rather than attempt to adjudicate on what is largely a matter of individual taste I have merely triple starred the age and strength category of the distillery concerned so that readers will be able to make their own enquiries and find out for themselves what else is offered beyond those described. From the particulars of the distilleries that follows in alphabetical order and from the Almanack of Scotch Whisky after that the reader should learn quite a lot about the making of malt whisky and the development of the industry itself.

The individual choice

Since all taste is a matter for the individual to make up his or her own mind about, it is impossible to do more than make suggestions and point the individual in the right direction. The basic information is here. It is up to each reader to go on as far as he wishes in his or her own way. It has often been argued that there is no such thing as bad Scotch whisky and it is up to everyone to make their own choice. There is certainly a great deal of satisfaction to be had from any Scotch whisky distilled in Scotland, but in the ensuing pages we are concerned with the original Scotch whisky which was distilled before the invention of the patent-still. In discovering the infinite variety and satisfaction to be had from the malt whiskies, distilled in the pot-stills of Scotland, the reader who has never sampled them before should find great enjoyment. Even those who have already grown to know and savour the flavours of the various malt whiskies may learn something from what follows. *Slainte!*

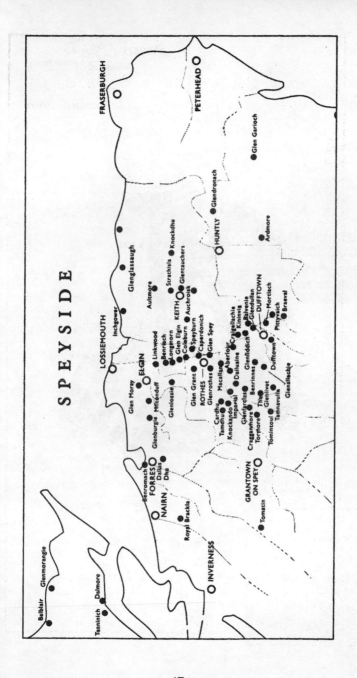

Distillery Groupings

(* Signifies generally available: nc, not commercially available; m, mothballed and not currently operational; c, closed

Allied-Domecq (Allied Distillers) Ardmore (Speyside nc), Glenburgie (Speyside nc), Glencadam (Highland, Eastern m. nc), *Glendronach (Speyside m.), *Glentauchers (Speyside), Imperial (Speyside m. nc), Inverleven (Lowland, Northern c.), *Laphroaig (Islay), Lochside. (Highland, Eastern c.), *Miltonduff (Speyside) *Tormore (Speyside), *Scapa (Orkney m.)

Angus Dundee Distillers plc. *Tomintoul (Speyside)

Bacardi, Ltd. (John Dewar & Sons) *Aberfeldy (Highland), *Aultmore (Speyside), *Craigellachie (Speyside), Macduff (*Glen Deveron: Speyside) *Royal Brackla (Highland, Northern)

Bladnoch Distillery, Ltd. Bladnoch. (Lowland, South West nc)

Burn Stewart Distillers plc. *Deanston (Highland, Southern), *Tobermory (*Ledaig, Island, Mull)

Diageo: (United Distillers & Vintners: UDV) Auchroisk (*The Singleton, Speyside), *Benrinnes (Speyside), *Blair Athol (Highland), *Cragganmore (Speyside), *Caol Isla (Islay), *Cardhu (Speyside), *Clynelish (Highland Northern), Coleburn (Speyside c), *Dailuaine (Speyside), *Dalwhinnie (Highland Central), *Dufftown-Glenlivet (Speyside), *Glen Elgin (Speyside), Glen Esk (Highland, Eastern c nc), *Glen Ord (Highland Northern), *Glen Spey (Speyside), *Glendullan (Speyside), *Glenkinchie (Lowland), *Glenlossie (Speyside), *Inchgower (Speyside), *Knockando (Speyside), *Lagavulin (Islay), *Linkwood (Speyside), *Mannochmore (Speyside), *Mortlach (Speyside), *Oban (Highland Western), Pittyvaich (Speyside c),, *Royal Lochnagar (Speyside), Strathmill (Speyside nc)*Teaninich (Highland, Northern), *Talisker (Island, Skye)

Edrington Group; (Highland Distillers Ltd., Robertson & Baxter, Ltd.) *Bunnahabhain (Islay), Glenglassaugh (Speyside c. nc), *Glengoyne (Highland, South West) *Glenrothes (Speyside), *Glenturret (Highland South), *Highland Park (Orkney), *Macallan (Speyside) *Tamdhu (Speyside)

Gordon & MacPhail, Ltd. *Benromach (Speyside nc)

J & G Grant *Glenfarclas (Speyside)

Wm Grant & Son *Balvenie (Speyside), Kininvie (Speyside nc), *Glenfiddich (Speyside) (Grain: Ladyburn, Girvan)

Inver House Distillers *Balblair (Highland, Northern), Balmenach (Speyside nc), Knockdhu (*An Cnoc, Speyside), Pulteney (*Old Pulteney, Highland, Northern), *Speyburn (Speyside)

Isle of Arran Distillers Ltd. *Isle of Arran (Island, Arran)

Jim Beam Brands (Worldwide) Inc. (JBB (Greater Europe) plc.) *Bruichladdich (Islay m), *Dalmore (Highland, Northern), *Fettercairn (Highland, East), *Isle of Jura (Island, Jura), Tamnavulin-Glenlivet (Speyside m), Tullibardine (Highland, Southern m) (Grain: *Invergordon)

Loch Lomond Distillery Co. Ltd. *Glen Scotia (Campbeltown), Littlemill (Lowland, West c), Loch Lomond (*Inchmurrin, *Old Rosdhu, Highland, South West) (Grain: Loch Lomond)

Glenmorangie plc. *Ardbeg (Islay), *Glen Moray (Speyside), *Glenmorangie (Highland, Northern)

J & A Mitchell *Springbank (*Longrow, Hazelburn, nc. (Campbeltown)

Nikka Whisky Distilling Co., Ltd., (Ben Nevis Distillery (Fort William) Ltd.) *Ben Nevis (Highland, Western)

Pernod Ricard (Campbell Distillers, Ltd.) *Aberlour (Speyside), *Edradour (Highland, Southern), Glenallachie (Speyside)

Seagram Distillers plc. Allt-a-Bhainne (Speyside nc), *Benriach (Speyside), Braeval (Speyside nc), Caperdonich (Speyside), *Glen Grant (Speyside), *The Glenlivet (Speyside), *Glen Keith (Speyside m), *Longmorn (Speyside), *Strathisla (Speyside)

Speyside Distillery Co. Ltd: Speyside (*Drumguish, *The Speyside, Speyside)

Suntory Group: (Morrison Bowmore Distillers Ltd,) *Auchentoshan (Lowland), *Bowmore (Islay), *Glen Garioch (Highland, Eastern)

Takara Shuzo: (Tomatin Distillery Co., Ltd) *Tomatin (Highland, Eastern)

A Directory of Malt Whiskies

ABERFELDY

Situation
Aberfeldy, Perthshire. 32 miles north-west of Perth. Tayside Region

Classification
Highland (Southern)

Origins and background
Built by the Dewar brothers, John and Tommy, in 1898 near where their father had been born. It may have been intended as a memorial to him, but was more probably seen as a seal on his and their success story, from crofters to distilling magnates in two generations. On their merger with the DCL in 1925 it became a part of the DCL empire, themselves merged into United Distillers when Guinness succeeded in their disputed take-over, but when they became Diageo and re-named their spirit division United Distillers & Vintners plc. (UDV) on their merger with Distillers & Vintners, the Monopolies Commission insisted they sold their Dewar holding. Hence in 1998 Aberfeldy was acquired by Bacardi Ltd. It now has a new £2 million Visitor Centre.

Owned by
John Dewar & Sons

Visitors
Reception Centre. Open all year. Tel: 01887 822 010: Fax: 01887 822 012

Age and strength when bottled
12 years at 40% volume.

Comments
Most still goes for blending in John Dewar's blends, but United Distillers wisely changed the old DCL policy and made most single malts available at the distilleries and selected outlets. Bacardi are continuing the policy. This is a peaty full-bodied highland single malt making a very good dram at any time.

ABERLOUR

Situation
Aberlour is near Ben Rinnes south-west of Keith, in the Spey Valley. Grampian Region

Classification
Highland (Speyside)

Origins and background
A distillery was first built near here in 1826 by James Gordon. The present distillery was built on the site in 1879 by a local banker, James Fleming. It was severely damaged by fire and was sold in 1892 to R. Thorne and Sons Ltd. who rebuilt and expanded it. It was bought by S. Campbell & Son Ltd in 1945 but in 1974 they were taken over by Pernod Ricard. Like so many Speyside distilleries, it is delightfully positioned close to the Spey and well screened from the road by a pine wood. Its water comes from the Well of St Drostan, which has connections with St Columba. The present distillery has been comprehensively modernised and as might be expected the malt whisky has been widely sold in France as well as the UK and USA.

Owned by
Campbell Distillers Ltd.

Visitors
By arrangement: Tel: 01340 871204

Age and strength when bottled*
10 and 15 years at 43% volume

Comments
This is a very good, clean post-prandial Speyside dram, full bodied and smooth and improving with age.

ALLT-A-BHAINNE (*alt-a-bane*)

Situation
4 miles south west of Dufftown on the slopes of Ben Rinnes.
Grampian Region

Classification
Highland (Speyside)

Origins and background
The name Allt-a-Bhainne means in Gaelic the milk burn,
signifying in this case perhaps a smooth malt whisky.
Opened in 1975 by Seagrams at a cost of £2.7 million this
distillery uses the most modern equipment and is very
carefully landscaped to fit in with the surrounding countryside. Its capacity of about one million proof gallons, or 2.595
million litres of alcohol, was doubled in 1989. This is one of
the latest distilleries to open in the region. Unfortunately it is
not sold as a single malt.

Owned by
Seagram Distillers plc

Visitors
By arrangement

Age and strength when bottled
Only bottled by the independent bottlers.

Comments
It seems a smooth clean dram, but it is difficult to judge when
only tasted in a 60% volume independent bottling.

AN CNOC *see* KNOCKDHU

ARDBEG

Situation
Port Ellen, on the south of Islay, Argyll. Strathclyde Region

Classification
Islay

Origins and background
Established by the McDougall family around 1815 on a site used originally for illicit distilling this distillery remained privately owned until taken over by Hiram Walker in 1979. The peaty water is obtained from two lochs inland from the distillery, Loch Arinambeast and Loch Uigeadale. The local barley and local peat are also used and production is only around 300,000 proof gallons a year, or 778,500 litres of alcohol, mostly used in blending. The stills are unusual, with a purifier attachment on the neck to return the higher alcohols for re-distillation, in effect triple distilling. The distillery was closed, but after Allied Distillers had taken over Hiram Walker it was re-opened in 1989, then later mothballed by Allied Distillers. Acquired by Glenmorangie plc. in 1998 and on stream again.

Owned by
Glenmorangie plc.

Visitors
Reception Centre: Open all year. Tel: 01496 302 244: Fax: 01496 302 040

Age and strength when bottled
10 years at 46% volume (non chill-filtered): 17 years at 40% volume.

Comments
A distinctively Islay malt, but perhaps due to the method of distillation, the 10 year old is light with a surprisingly delicate aftermath, a dram to savour. The 17 year old has the full peaty iodine body of the south Islay malts (Lagavulin and Laphroaig) with a very long aftermath which you either like greatly or hate.

ARDMORE

Situation
At Kennethmont, 17 miles south of Huntly. Grampian Region

Classification
Highland (Speyside)

Origins and background
Built by William Teacher's sons in 1891 when they realised the importance of having their own direct access to supplies of malt whisky for blending purposes. It was modernised and greatly enlarged in the 1950s, when William Teacher remained one of the largest independent whisky distillers still in the control of the original family. Taken over in 1976 by Allied Breweries who in 1988 were acquired in turn by Allied-Lyons, who formed Allied Distillers Ltd., now part of Allied-Domecq.

Owned by
Allied Distillers

Visitors
By arrangement

Age and strength when bottled
Only a Centenary bottling: 12 year old at 40% volume

Comments
This has always been retained by William Teacher and Sons as the basis for their famous blend and only a little found its way onto the market through the independent bottlers. The centenary bottling is a very recognisably Speyside malt, clean and fresh, with a full body and good aftermath. It should be more available

ARRAN *see* ISLE OF ARRAN

AUCHENTOSHAN

Situation
Ten miles north of Glasgow at Duntocher, Dunbartonshire.
Strathclyde Region

Classification
Lowland

Origins and background
Established in 1825 on the road from Glasgow to Dumbarton
it was badly damaged by bombs during the 1939-45 War but
was completely rebuilt and modernised. Acquired in 1984 by
Stanley P. Morrison Ltd, then still a private company, but
now owned by Morrison, Bowmore Distillers Ltd., part in
turn of Suntory. (See Bowmore and Glen Garioch.) It lies just
below the 'Highland Line' so the whisky is technically a
Lowland malt although peat and water are obtained from
north of the 'Line'. The latter is from Loch Cochno in the
Kilpatrick Hills. The distilling process is unusual in that three
stills are used instead of the customary two. The whisky is
therefore triple-distilled and possibly this may be responsible for producing a lighter malt than usual.

Owned by
Morrison Bowmore Distillers Ltd

Visitors
No

Age and strength when bottled
'Select' (Unaged) and 10 years at 40% volume: 21 years at
43% volume

Comments
Perhaps due to the triple distillation the unaged 'Select' is a
light and clean tasting dram. The 10 year old is also a good
dram with more body and depth and the 21 year old is
extremely smooth.

AUCHROISK

Situation
Mulben, Banffshire. Grampian Region

Classification
Highland (Speyside)

Origins and background
Auchroisk is somewhat unusual, being newly built in 1974 by the International Distillers and Vintners Ltd, and taking its name from a nearby farm, the Gaelic meaning of which is 'the ford over the red stream'. The water for the distillery is drawn from a spring known as Dorie's Well which provides an ample supply. As might be expected the buildings are extremely modern but blend well with the countryside. This amounted to a multi-million pound investment and the eight stills have a production capacity of 1.6 million gallons, or 7.3 million litres of alcohol. The malt whisky is marketed under the name **The Singleton** on the pretext that Auchroisk is not easily pronounced.

Owned by
UDV

Visitors
No; by arrangement only. Tel: 01542 860333

Age and strength when bottled
10 years old at 40% and 43% volume

Comments
Although a modern distillery the malt whisky produced is a pleasing, smooth after-dinner dram with a good aftermath. Clearly a lot must go for blending, but it is readily available.

AULTMORE

Situation
About 3 miles from Keith and 9 miles from Buckie. Grampian Region

Classification
Highland (Speyside)

Origins and background
The distillery was originally built in 1896 by Alexander Edward of Sanquhar obtaining water from the Auchinderran burn. In 1899 as M/D of a company with the resounding title of The Oban and Aultmore Glenlivet Distillery Co. Ltd, Alexander Edward relinquished ownership to the newly formed Company, which controlled both distilleries. In the hard times of 1923 Aultmore was acquired by John Dewar & Sons Ltd. In 1925 it then became part of DCL, re-named United Distillers plc in 1988 under overall control of Guinness plc., but, after their 1997 merger with Distillers and Vintners, when United Distillers and Vinters (UDV) was formed, in 1998 Aultmore passed to Bacardi. Until 1969 it was still powered by a steam engine.

Owned by
John Dewar & Sons

Visitors
No

Age and strength when bottled
12 years old at 43% volume

Comments
At one time sold as being in 'the longest glen in Scotland' it no longer flaunts the misleading Glenlivet affix and has no need to do so. Although a lot goes for blending this malt whisky is readily available and makes a very good after-dinner drink. It is a good smooth dram with a clean dry aftermath.

BALBLAIR

Situation
Edderton, near Tain, Ross-shire. Highland Region

Classification
Highland (Northern)

Origins and background
Dating back to 1790, or possibly even earlier to around 1750, this distillery may claim to be amongst the oldest in Scotland. The distillery on the present site, however, dates from 1872 when it was very greatly developed by Andrew Ross & Son, the owners at that time. Edderton is well supplied with both ample peat and water, which is of course a considerable asset to the distillery. It was bought by Hiram Walker in 1969 and another still added. In 1988 it became part of Allied Distillers, but was acquired by Inver House Distillers in 1996. It is a good example of a fast maturing malt whisky.

Owned by
Inver House Distillers

Visitors
No: By appointment only

Age and strength when bottled
'Elements' unaged at 40% volume: 16 years at 40% volume;

Comments
Much of this malt whisky still goes for blending, but the unaged 'Elements,' is a pleasing light and rather dry dram with clean aftermath. The 16 year old, as might be expected, has a good deal more body and a longer slightly peaty aftermath making a good after dinner dram.

BALMENACH

Situation
Balmenach, Cromdale, Grantown-on-Spey, Morayshire.
Grampian Region

Classification
Highland (Speyside)

Origins & Background
Founded in 1801 by illicit distiller James MacGregor but the
distillery officially dates from 1824 when he took out a
license . As well as founding the distillery and running it
for many years he was the grandfather of Robert Bruce
Lockhart who describes it delightfully in his book, *Scotch*.
In the same great storm of 28th December 1879 which caused
the Tay Bridge disaster the distillery chimney stack col-
lapsed. There was nearly a fire but the stillman saved the
day by opening the discharge cocks allowing the spirit to run
out and preventing the fire spreading. In 1897 the grandson
of the founder formed the Balmenach-Glenlivet Distillery
Ltd, adding the affix Glenlivet, since dropped. In 1922
during the lean post-war years control passed to DCL Closed
in 1993, it was acquired by Inver House Distillers in 1998.
This fast developing and enterprising Scottish group
promptly spent £250,000 renovating the distillery and this
excellent single malt should soon be widely available again.

Owned by
Inver House Distillers

Visitors
No

Age and strength when bottled
Not currently bottled as a single malt.

Comments
Unfortunately still only available through independent bottlings. From various tastings, however, it seems a very
interesting after-dinner dram, which should soon become
available again.

BALVENIE

Situation
Dufftown, Banffshire. Grampian Region

Classification
Highland (Speyside)

Origins and background
Dufftown is now rated as Scotland's whisky capital since the eclipse of Campbeltown. A local jingle runs:
'Rome was built on seven hills
Dufftown stands on seven stills.'
The distillery was established in 1892 by William Grant on part of the land he had bought for his nearby Glenfiddich distillery. The water for distilling is obtained from the fine Robbie Dhu springs and both distilleries use the nearby Fiddich Burn for cooling purposes. Still owned by the firm of William Grant & Sons Ltd, the distillery was greatly expanded in 1955. It still has its own maltings which supply about 10% of the total malt used.

Owned by
William Grant & Sons Ltd

Visitors
No

Age and strength when bottled***
The Balvenie Founders Reserve is a vatting of distillates from casks of between 10 and 12 years at 40% volume. Balvenie Double Wood is vatted at 12 years and 40% volume. The Balvenie Port Wood after 21 years in bourbon casks is finished in port casks at 40% volume.

Comments
All are exceptional very smooth drams, improving with age, with no resemblance to nearby Glenfiddich.

BEN NEVIS

Situation
Ben Nevis, Fort William, Inverness-shire. Highland Region

Classification
Highland (Western)

Origins and background
Built in 1825 by 'Long John' Macdonald, a local farmer turned distiller, noted for his outstanding size and physique. He presented Queen Victoria with a cask of Ben Nevis malt whisky on her visit to Fort William in 1848 and on his death in 1856 was succeeded by his son Donald, followed in turn by his son John. In 1941 the distillery was acquired by Joseph Hobbs owner of the Great Glen, who added a grain still, but in 1978 it was closed. In 1981 it was bought by Long John International Ltd, a Seager Evans subsidiary, and Whitbread & Co, Ltd. In 1984 distilling re-started, but ceased again in 1986. In 1989 it was acquired by the Nikka Whisky Distilling Co., Ltd, founded by Masataka Taketsura, who married a Scots girl in 1920 while studying distilling at Glasgow University and subsequently at Campbeltown. Among the first to distil malt whisky in Japan, he worked as expert adviser to Suntory in their malt whisky distillery before setting up on his own in 1934. Distilling at Ben Nevis started again in 1990 under Colin Ross, M/D of the Ben Nevis Distillery (Fort William) Ltd.

Owned by
Ben Nevis Distillery (Fort William) Ltd

Visitors
Reception centre. Open all year. Tel: 01397 700200: Fax: 01397 702768

Age and strength when bottled
10 years and 46% volume.

Comments
This ten year old Highland malt has fullness and body with a good aftermath making it a good dram at any time.

BENRIACH

Situation
Next to Longmorn just south of Elgin, Morayshire.
Grampian Region

Classification
Speyside

Origins and background
Built by John Duff next to the Longmorn distillery.in 1898
with plentiful supplies of local spring water and peat from
Mannoch Hill. With the collapse of the whisky market it was
closed down in 1900. In 1965 it was completely re-built with
four stills by The Glenlivet Distillers, now part of Seagram
and has been producing a very good whisky since then,
mostly for blending.

Owned by
Seagram Distillers plc

Visitors
By arrangement.

Age and strength when bottled
10 years and 43% volume

Comments
Although close to Longmorn, very different, but still light
and extremely delicate. Most goes for blending, but it is now
bottled and available in various outlets. A good pre-prandial
dram.

BENRINNES

Situation
Benrinnes, Aberlour, Banffshire. Grampian Region

Classification
Highland (Speyside)

Origins and background
Naturally the distillery is named after nearby Ben Rinness from which it obtains its water supplies. It was built in 1897 towards the very end of the Scotch whisky boom and operated successfully and independently until the lean years after the First World War. It was then acquired by John Dewar & Sons Ltd who took it over under their name in 1926. With their take-over by DCL it was transferred to the Scottish Malt Distillers Ltd. It has continued operating since then except for very brief closures at the start of the 1930s and in 1943 during the last War. In the mid-1950s it was extensively re-built and in the mid-1960s the number of stills doubled from three to six.

Owned by
UDV

Visitors
No

Age and strength when bottled
15 years at 43% volume

Comments
Previously obtainable only through the independent bottlers, but owing to United Distillers sensible change of policy, it is now available from the distillery and selected outlets and makes a very pleasing aperitif with a delicate dry peaty aftermath.

BENROMACH

Situation
Just north of Forres, Morayshire. Grampian Region

Classification
Highland (Speyside)

Origins and background
Built in 1898 by Duncan McCallum of the Glen Nevis Distillery and Leith spirit broker F.W.Brickman, and obtaining its water from the nearby Chapeltown springs. From 1907 run by McCallum alone. After 1918 revived as the Benromach Distillery Ltd., but closed from 1931 to 1936. Acquired by Associated Scottish Distillers Ltd in 1938, and sold to DCL in 1953. It was renovated and re-built in 1966 with two stills, but closed and dismantled in the 1983. Bought by Gordon & MacPhail in 1993 and by 1998 restored, with two short-necked stills designed to produce a full rich spirit, when, opened by HRH the Prince of Wales, it came on stream again with a capacity of 500,000 litres.

Owned by
Gordon & MacPhail

Visitors
By arrangement: Open all year. Tel: 01309 675968

Age and Strength when bottled***
Not as yet stated, but a 15 year old at 40% is available

Comments
By 2008 it should be possible to taste this addition to Gordon & MacPhail's wide range of malt whisky bottlings. The 15 year old is a clean, light and satisfying dram.

BLADNOCH

Situation
1 mile south-east of Wigtown. Dumfries & Galloway egion

Classification
Lowland (South West)

Origins
This most southerly of all the Scottish malt distilleries was founded in 1817 by the McClelland family on the river at the lower end of Bladnoch village from which it takes its name. It has had a somewhat varied history with three distinct periods of expansion followed by temporary closures. After changing hands a number of times it was finally closed for 18 years from the start of the 1939-45 War years, during which period it even had the stills removed and sent to Sweden. It was only re-opened in 1956, changing hands several more times until bought by Arthur Bell & Sons in 1983 from Inverhouse Distillers Ltd, hence then controlled by United Distillers plc. In 1994 it was acquired by the Armstrong family, and opened as a Heritage Centre, but in 2000 re-started limited distilling.

Owned by
Bladnoch Distillery Ltd.

Visitors
Visitor Centre: Open all year. Weekdays: 9.30-5.00. Tel 01988 402235: Fax: 01988 402605:

Age and strength when bottled
10 years at 43% volume

Comments
This lowland malt whisky is a very pleasing smooth dram with a light clean flavour and surprising aftermath. It is good that the southernmost Scots distillery is operating again even part-time.

BLAIR ATHOL

Situation
Pitlochry, Perthshire. Tayside Region

Classification
Highland (Central)

Origins and background
Founded in 1825 this distillery obtains its water from the Allt Dour, the burn of the Otter, and the mountain springs of Ben Vrackie above Pitlochry. Although misleadingly named after the village close to the ducal seat at Blair Castle it has an attractive position in this well-known tourist centre. It was initially run by Alexander Connacher & Co., but was acquired by P. Mackenzie & Co., Distillers Ltd, of Edinburgh, who greatly enlarged it. After the lean 1914-18 War years it was closed until bought by Arthur Bell & Sons Ltd, in 1949 when it was rebuilt. In 1973 the number of stills was doubled from two to four. Since 1988 controlled by United Distillers, now UDV.

Owned by
UDV

Visitors
Reception Centre. Open all year. Times vary. Tel: 01796 482003 Fax: 01796 482001

Age and strength when bottled
12 years at 43% volume

Comments
A lot of this is no doubt used for blending by Arthur Bell & Sons, but it is readily available as a malt whisky. It is an interesting full-bodied dry dram with very little aftermath which makes a good drink before a meal.

BOWMORE

Situation
On the north of the Isle of Islay, on the shore of Loch Indaal and actually right on the sea.

Classification
West Coast Islay

Origins and background
Bowmore was founded in 1779 by a Mr Simpson and is the oldest distillery on Islay obtaining its' water from the river Laggan, possibly not as peaty a source as the southern Islay distilleries of Ardbeg, Laphroaig and Lagavulin. It was expanded by a James Mutter in the late 19th century until the 1890s when it was taken over by the Bowmore Distillery Co. Ltd. Bought by Stanley P.Moprrison in 1963, control then passed to the Morrison Bowmore Distillers Ltd., subject of a management buy-out in 1989. At that time Suntory had a 35% holding and in 1994 took full control, the first and still foremost Japanese distillers of malt whisky, now with the largest stake in the Scotch Whisky industry.

Owned by
Morrison Bowmore Distillers Ltd.

Visitors
Reception centre. Open all year. Tel and Fax: 01496 810671

Age and strength when bottled***
'Legend' (unaged) and 12 years at 40% volume and 15, 17, 21, 25 and 30 years at 43% volume

Comments
A smooth and pleasing after-dinner Islay malt whisky, without the heaviness of the southern Islay malts but with a distinct character of its own and increasing in authority with age.

BRACKLA *see* ROYAL BRACKLA

BRAEVAL

Situation
9 miles south west of Dufftown, above Chapeltown of Glenlivet, Grampian Region

Classification
Highland (Speyside)

Origins and background
Built in 1973 by Seagram Distillers plc and then named Braes of Glenlivet. The reason for building it was to acquire the Glenlivet affix and it had in fact good grounds for the addition, being closer to the Glenlivet distillery than any other. Although the design is fairly traditional, with non-functional pagoda-style roof, it naturally employs all the latest engineering and production techniques. It has a capacity of over a million proof gallons a year or 2.595 million litres of alcohol. Two wells close by, the Preenie and Kate's Well, provide the water supply for the distilling process. When Seagram Distillers plc acquired The Glenlivet Distillers in 1978 the need for a competing Glenlivet name disappeared and after a process of 'rationalisation' the name was changed in 1994 to Braeval, the name of the croft on which it was built.

Owned by
Seagram Distillers plc

Visitors
By arrangement

Age and strength when bottled
All is used for blending, but some is sometimes bottled by the independent bottlers.

Comments
This should be a very interesting malt whisky if any was freed for consumption by the public and with the change of name, it is rational that a further change of policy may follow.

BRORA *see* CLYNELISH

BRUICHLADDICH (*brewichladdie*)

Situation
Bruichladdich, Isle of Islay, Argyll. Strathclyde Region

Classification
Islay

Origins and background
This is the most westerly distillery in Scotland right on the sea. It was built in 1881 by the Harvey family, well known distillers, who formed John and Robert Harvey Limited. From 1886 onwards they ran their Islay distillery as the Bruichladdich Distillery Co. (Islay) Ltd, and it continued thus until its closure in 1938 and acquisition ultimately by the National Distillers of America, who controlled it through a holding company Train & McIntyre, who in turn incorporated it into their distilling side, Associated Scottish Distillers. After further changes of ownership the distillery was acquired by Invergordon Distillers Ltd in 1968 who added two new stills and general expansion so that it now has a capacity of 800,000 proof gallons or 2,076,000 litres of alcohol. Its water supplies are obtained from an inland reservoir. It was acquired by Whyte & Mackay in 1993, mothballed in 1995 and re-opened in 1998.

Owned by
JBB (Greater Europe) plc.

Visitors
No

Age and strength when bottled***
10, 15 and 21 years at 40% volume

Comments
Perhaps because its water supply comes from inland this is not like many other Islay malt whiskies. It is a very good aperitif, light and peaty and although a very pleasing dram it is not as heavy as others on Islay.

BUNNAHABHAIN (*bunahavan*)

Situation
Bunnahabhain, Port Askaig, on the south of the Isle of Islay, Argyll. Strathclyde Region

Classification
Islay

Origins and background
Built on the north-east coast of Islay and obtaining water from the river Margadale, Bunnahabhain started distilling in 1883. The Islay Distillery Co., which controlled the distillery, merged in 1887 to become part of the Highland Distillers Ltd. In 1963 the distillery was enlarged from two to four stills. In 1970 Highland Distillers took over the notable blend The Famous Grouse along with Matthew Gloag & Son Ltd. and then expanded remarkably. Until the 1990s almost all the product of the distillery went for blending. In 1999 they were acquired by the Scottish based Edrington Group.

Owned by
Highland Distillers Ltd.

Visitors
Reception Centre. Open all year. Tel: 01496 840 646: Fax: 01496 840 248

Age and strength when bottled
12 years at 40% volume

Comments
A good after-dinner dram, but lighter than the northern Islay malt whiskies. While it has a full-bodied and distinctive flavour it leaves a very pleasing aftermath and is now widely available.

CAOL ILA (*coal eela*)

Situation
Caol Ila, Port Askaig, on the east of the Isle of Islay, Argyll.
Strathclyde Region

Classification
Islay

Origins and background
Possibly founded around 1846 Caol Ila is situated in the most
sheltered bay on Islay east of Port Askaig and overlooking
the Sound of Jura. It has its own private wharf through
which it obtains its own barley and ships off its whisky in
return. It gets its water supplies from the peaty waters of
Loch nam Ban, said to be the finest on Islay. The owners from
1880 to 1920 were Bulloch Lade & Co. Ltd, who were a
subsidiary of Robertson & Baxter Ltd. In 1920 they formed
Caol Ila Distillery Co. Ltd, to run the distillery. When DCL
took them over in 1927 the management reverted to Bulloch
Lade & Co. Ltd. Only a limited amount is available on the
home market, apart from the independent bottlers, but it is
available overseas under the name Glen Isla.

Owned by
UDV

Visitors
Reception Centre. Tel: 01496 302760; Fax 01496 302763

Age and strength when bottled
12 years old at 40% volume

Comments
A very light coloured pleasing pre-prandial dram, not as full
bodied as many on Islay, but with an attractive peaty aftermath.

CAPERDONICH

Situation
Rothes, Morayshire. Grampian Region

Classification
Highland (Speyside)

Origins and background
In 1897 Major James Grant, son of Elgin lawyer, James Grant, founder of the Glen Grant distillery at Rothes, decided to build a second distillery across the road from the first named Glen Grant 2, joining the two distilleries by a pipe, which mixed the two malts produced. Following the crash of the 1890s the No. 2 distillery was closed down in 1901. It was rebuilt in 1965 and renamed the Caperdonich Distillery Ltd, using the name of the Caperdonich Well from which the water was obtained for the original Glen Grant distillery, and which has never been known to run dry. In 1967 it was enlarged from two to four stills.

Owned by
Seagram Distillers plc

Visitors
By arrangement

Age and strength when bottled
Only available from the independent bottlers so varies

Comments
Similar, hardly surprisingly, to its neighbour Glen Grant, if not, perhaps, in quite the same class, although since only available via independent bottlings it is hard to say. It seems to be a pleasing enough dram with a good aftermath. It is a pity that it is not more readily available.

CARDHU (*cardoo*)

Situation
Knockando, Morayshire. Grampian Region

Classification
Highland (Speyside)

Origins and background
Founded in 1824 by John Cummings on a site where he had distilled whisky illicitly for many years. A second distillery close by was built in 1855, when the first had fallen into disrepair. It was bought by John Walker & Sons Ltd in 1893. Its' water supply is piped from Mannoch Hill two miles to the north-west and the distillery also gets its peat from the same site. It was extensively modernised in 1965 and expanded from four to six stills. The whisky is known as Cardhu. (Gaelic for black rock) The distillery was often known as Cardow, which is merely a different spelling of the nearby hamlet sited on the banks of the Spey. Now part of UDV.

Owned by
UDV

Visitors
Reception Centre. Open all year. Tel: 01340 872555: 01340 872556

Age and strength when bottled
12 years at 40% volume

Comments
Smooth and clean with a good slightly sweet aftermath this is a very sound after-dinner Speyside malt whisky.

CLYNELISH (*clyne-leesh*)

Situation
Brora, Sutherland. Highland Region

Classification
Highland (Northern)

Origins and background
Originally built in 1819 as a model of its kind by the Duke of Sutherland, then Marquis of Stafford, to provide a market for the grain of the crofters forcibly moved to the coast as a result of the Clearances.and leased to James Harper from Midlothian In the ensuing years the whisky produced was much prized. Subsequently in 1896 James Ainslie & Co. took over the distillery and completely rebuilt it. Despite the collapse of the whisky boom at the turn of the century James Ainslie & Co. continued in business until 1912 when the DCL acquired a considerable shareholding. and The Clynelish Distillery Co. Ltd was formed. In 1925 DCL took over completely. During the 1930s slump and the 1939 War the distillery was closed,. In 1967 it was .re-built with six stills on an adjacent site using water from the same source, the Clynemilton burn The original distillery, at first known as Clynelish 'B', was renamed the 'Brora' distillery and from 1969 to 1983 produced a highly regarded single malt. Sadly it has now closed and is a Visitor Centre.

Owned by
UDV

Visitors
Reception Centre. Open all year. Times vary. Tel: 01408 623000 Fax: 01408 623004

Age and strength when bottled
12 years at 40% volume

Comments
A rather peaty and very interesting after-dinner dram with an extremely good aftermath.

COLEBURN

Situation
Longmorn, by Elgin, Morayshire. Grampian Region

Classification
Highland (Speyside)

Origins and background
The distillery was built in 1896 by John Robertson & Son Ltd,
trying like many others to cash in on the seemingly ever
upwards spiral of the Scotch whisky boom of the nineties.
During the early years of the present century the distillery
was the subject of several successful experiments in the
purification of industrial effluents. The process developed
at Coleburn was utilised in a number of distilleries elsewhere
in the area. The distillery was taken over in 1916 by the
Clynelish Distillery Co. Ltd, and in 1930 it was acquired by
the Scottish Malt Distillers Ltd, a subsidiary of the DCL. The
malt produced was mostly used for distilling but some was
bottled by the independent bottlers. It has been closed since
1985 and seems unlikely to re-open.

Owned by
UDV

Visitors
No

Age and strength when bottled
Only available through the independent bottlers

Comments
In view of the proximity of a malt whisky such as Longmorn
it seems a pity this has not been bottled by the distillery.
Judging by two independent bottlings it seems an interesting
light and clean tasting dram, even if not up to its neighbour's
standards.

CRAGGANMORE

Situation
Ballindalloch, Banffshire. Grampian Region

Classification
Highland (Speyside)

Origins and background
Taking its water from the Craggan burn, the distillery was built in 1869 by John Smith, who had left his employer at The Glenlivet Distillery to branch out on his own account as a self-employed farmer and distiller. A man of considerable strength and magnificent physique he is reputed to have moved a large stone which stands at the entrance to the distillery by his own efforts when it obstructed his plough. In the course of so doing he uncovered a hidden treasure and flourished exceedingly thereafter. His son Gordon Smith inherited the distillery from his father and on his death in 1923 it was sold to a syndicate who formed the Cragganmore Distillery Co. Ltd. A leading member of the syndicate was Peter J. Mackie, later Sir Peter Mackie, of White Horse Distillers Ltd. In the mid-1960s the distillery was extended from four to six stills and DCL bought out the remaining shareholders, hence it is now part of United Distillers & Vintners.

Owned by
UDV

Visitors
By arrangement: Tel: 01807 500202

Age and strength when bottled***
12 years at 40% volume

Comments
Although the bulk still goes for blending it is now readily available and marketed as one of UDV's six 'Classic Malts'. It is a good dry and demanding after-dinner dram, possibly more west-coast in character rather than typically Speyside.

CRAIGELLACHIE

Situation
Craigellachie, Banffshire. Grampian Region

Classification
Highland (Speyside)

Origins and background
Built in 1890 by Peter J. Mackie in partnership with Alexander Edward, as the Craigellachie-Glenlivet Distillery Ltd, but eventually taken over completely by Peter Mackie. It stands impressively above the well known single-span Craigellachie bridge across the River Spey and the Craigellachie Rock Its' water comes from a spring on Little Conval hill. When Mackie & Co., Distillers, Ltd, were taken over in 1924 by the DCL to be transformed into White Horse Distillers Limited, the distillery became part of the DCL. In 1998 it was acquired by Bacardi following a Monopolies Commission investigation.

Owned by
John Dewar &Sons

Visitors
No

Age and strength when bottled
14 years at 43% volume

Comments
This is another single malt, which United Distillers started bottling and selling on a limited basis. Now readily available it is a light and clean after-dinner dram.

DAILUAINE

Situation
Carron, Morayshire. Grampian Region

Classification
Highland (Speyside)

Origins and background
The distillery was built in the shadow of Ben Rinnes in 1852, obtaining water from the Bailliemullich burn, but was completely renovated and rebuilt at the start of the whisky boom in the early 1890s by Thomas Mackenzie. A merger between Daluaine-Glenlivet Distillers Ltd, and Talisker Distillery Ltd, in 1898 led to the formation of the Daluaine-Talisker Distilleries Ltd. They were acquired in 1916 jointly by Dewar, DCL, W. P. Lowrie and Johnnie Walker, before all came under the DCL umbrella in 1925. Completely re-built again in 1960 and extended from four to six stills.

Owned by
UDV

Visitors
No

Age and strength when bottled
16 years at 43% volume

Comments
Yet another single malt which United Distillers started bottling on a limited scale. It provides an extremely interesting smooth dram, which is well worth making an effort to find.

DALMORE

Situation
Alness, Ross-shire. Highland Region

Classification
Highland (Northern)

Origins and background
Splendidly placed overlooking the Black Isle and the Cromarty Firth, with the sole rights to take water from the river Alness, the Dalmore distillery was founded in 1839 by Alexander Matheson of the Hong Kong trading company Jardine Matheson but taken over by Mackenzie Brothers in 1867. Although they merged with Whyte & Mackay Ltd in 1960 they had a Mackenzie of the third generation serving on the board until 1988 when Whyte &Mackay was sold by Lonrho to Brent Walker. While one of the stills in use dates back to 1874 the distillery has a record of adopting modern methods of production and its capacity is 1.2 million gallons, or 3.114 million litres of alcohol. During the 1914-18 War the distillery was taken over by the Royal Navy for assembling mines and did not start distilling again until 1922. In 1990 Whyte & Mackay was acquired by Gallaghers Tobacco, plc., a subsidiary of American Brands, Inc. and now of Jim Beam Brands (Worldwide) Inc. The bulk goes into Whyte & Mackay's blends, but some is bottled and well marketed.

Owned
JBB(Greater Europe) plc.

Visitors
By arrangement: Tel: 01349 882362

Age and strength when bottled***
12, 15 and 21 years at 40% volume

Comments
A rather dry but very pleasing heavy after-dinner dram with an interesting aftermath increasing in authority with age.

DALWHINNIE

Situation
Dalwhinnie, Inverness-shire. Highland Region below Aviemore

Classification
Highland (Central)

Origins and background
Sited in the Pass of Drumochter, the distillery was built in 1898 by Alex Mackenzie and George Sellar of Kingussie at a height of 1,174 feet and it was then claimed to be the highest distillery in Scotland. The Gaelic meaning of Dalwhinnie is 'the meeting place' and it is certainly an area which has lived up to its name over the centuries. Historically it has seen clan battles and Prince Charles' army encamped after the raising of the standard at Glenfinnan in 1745 as he marched down General Wade's military road, which runs through the distillery grounds. The distillery was taken over from the founders by A. P. Blyth & Son who sold it in 1905 to James Munro & Son Ltd, an American syndicate. In 1921 it was sold to Sir James Calder and in 1926 was taken over by J & G Stewart Ltd, but in 1930 went to the Scottish Malt Distillers Ltd, under DCL control. It was mostly used for blending but now promoted very successfully as one of the UDV's six 'Classic Malts'.

Owned by
UDV

Visitors
Reception Centre. Open all year. Tel: 01450 672219: Fax: 01450 672228

Age and strength when bottled***
15 years at 43% volume

Comments
Well-marketed and widely available, as a UDV 'Classic Malt' this is a fresh but very smooth malt whisky with a good clean aftermath. A pleasing dram. to be drunk at any time of the day.

DEANSTON

Situation
Doune, Perthshire. Tayside Region

Classification
Highland (Southern)

Origins & background
Sited in the Trossachs on the banks of the Teith, a salmon river which provides its' water, and named after the nearby village of Deanston, this distillery is a mile from picturesque Castle Doune. Built as a cotton mill in 1785, when closed by the mill-owners, James Finlay & Co. Ltd, in 1965 Mr Brodie Hepburn, well-known in the whisky industry, saw the potential of large premises well placed on the Teith, with a water turbine and stand-by generator in working order. He proposed conversion into a distillery and agreed a deal whereby James Finlay& Co., Ltd., took two thirds of the equity and Brodie Hepburn Ltd the remainder and overall control. Two wash and two spirit stills were installed and in 1969 production started. In 1972 Deanston Distillers Ltd., was taken over by Invergordon Distillers Ltd, but closed in 1982. In 1991 it was sold to Burn Stewart & Co. Ltd. and distilling re-started. It has a capacity of 2,800,000 litres of alcohol.

Owned by
Burn Stewart & Co., Ltd.

Visitors
No

Age and strength when bottled
12 years at 40% volume: 17 and 25 years at 40% and 43% volume

Comments
The 12 year old is a clean pre-dinner dram light, fresh and a touch sweet, growing smoother and mellower with age.

DUFFTOWN-GLENLIVET

Situation
Dufftown, Banffshire. Grampian Region

Classification
Highland (Speyside)

Origins and background
Built in 1896 by P. Mackenzie & Co., Distillers, Ltd, just to the south of Dufftown in the Dullan Glen this is another distillery using the hyphenated Glenlivet affix. Despite the fact that the Dullan and Fiddich burns both flow down the Dullan Glen to the Spey, it obtains its water supplies from 'Jock's Well' in the nearby Conval hills regarded as ideal for distilling purposes and noted for its never-failing supply of fine water. In 1933 the distillery was acquired by Arthur Bell & Sons Ltd, at the start of their steady expansion and this was to become one of the principal sources of their popular blend. It now has six stills and is a subsidiary of UDV.

Owned by
UDV

Visitors
No

Age and strength when bottled
8 and 10 years at 40% volume

Comments
A light but smooth, very typical Speyside malt whisky and a good aperitif. The 8 year old, hardly surprisingly, is not quite up to the standard of the 10 year old. They may feel they need the Glenlivet affix, but both are sound enough on their own merits.

DRUMGUISH *see* SPEYSIDE

EDRADOUR

Situation
Pitlochry, Perthshire. Tayside Region

Classification
Highland (Southern)

Origins and background
Believed to have been founded around 1825 by a group of local farmers the present distillery was probably built around 1837 using water from a spring on Ben Vrackie. For many years owned by John McIntosh & Co. it was sold to William Whiteley & Co. Ltd in 1933, a firm acquired in 1938 by Mr Irving Haim, an American, until, forty years on, in 1978 control passed to Mr Delbert Coleman, a U.S financier, whose holding company was J. G. Turney Ltd. In 1982 the distillery was taken over by Pernod Ricard, through their subsidiary S. Campbell & Son Ltd, and they are the current owners. It lies beside a burn with steep banks on land leased from the Duke of Atholl. Among the most attractively placed distilleries in Scotland, it is certainly the smallest. The spirit still holds under 500 gallons and production rarely exceeds 1,000 gallons a week. More than almost any other distillery it resembles the way a highland distillery was worked in the 19th century. It only employs three men, but they manage the entire operation efficiently and smoothly making this distillery a pleasure to visit. Pernod Ricard are to be congratulated on not having made any alterations to this showpiece distillery.

Owned by
Campbell Distillers Ltd.

Visitors
Reception Centre. Shut January/February. Tel: 01796 472095: Fax: 01796 472002

Age and strength when bottled
10 years at 40%

Comments
A good clean smooth and light malt whisky with a pleasing aftermath, also bottled by the independent bottlers.

FETTERCAIRN

Situation
Fettercairn, Kincardineshire. Grampian Region

Classification
Highland (East)

Origins and background
The exact date of origin is uncertain but the present distillery
was known to be functioning in 1824 and continued distilling
under various owners until it was taken over by a local landowner Sir John Gladstone, brother of the Prime Minister. Sir
John formed the Fettercairn Distillery Co. in 1887. It underwent
a long period of closure from the First World War onward until
it was bought by the Associated Scottish Distillers Ltd in 1939
for Train & McIntyre. It then passed to Mr Tom Scott Sutherland, an Aberdonian business man, who retained it until 1971
when it was purchased jointly by Hay and MacLeod & Co. and
W. & S. Strong & Co. It is now an up-to-date modern distillery
with water in plenty from the nearby Grampian Mountains
and four stills. Situated in the fertile Howe o' the Mearns it has
plentiful barley supplies at hand. The capacity is about 500,000
proof gallons. The malt whisky produced is known as **Old
Fettercairn**. Much goes for blending, but it is well marketed.

Owned by
JBB (Greater Europe) plc

Visitors
Reception Centre. May to September. Tel: 01561 340205: Fax:
01561 340547

Age and strength when bottled***
10 years at 40% volume

Comments
Perhaps not as widely appreciated as it deserves to be, this is
a good clean, dry and satisfying malt whisky which makes a
pleasing dram before dinner.

GLEN DEVERON *see* MACDUFF

GLEN ELGIN

Situation
Longmorn, Elgin, Morayshire: Grampian Region

Classification
Highland (Speyside)

Origins and background
It cannot be often that bankers get together to found a distillery and it is entirely suitable that this should happen on Speyside where banking, salmon and whisky might all be considered local industries. In 1900 Mr James Carle and Mr W. Simpson, both bankers in Elgin, founded this distillery at Longmorn near Glen Rothes in as pleasant a position as any in the Highlands. It obtains its water supplies from springs in Glen Rothes. The Glen Elgin-Glenlivet Distillery Co. Ltd, another hyphenated Glenlivet distillery company, was formed to run the venture. Then in 1907 J. J. Blanche of Glasgow took over the company, but in 1936 it was finally acquired by the Scottish Malt Distillers.

Owned by
UDV

Visitors
By arrangement. Tel: 01343 860212

Age and strength when bottled
12 years at 43% volume

Comments
The bulk is used for blending, but some is regularly bottled and sold. It is a typical clean Speyside dram with a light but pleasing aftermath. This is a good single malt whisky which may be drunk at any time with enjoyment.

GLEN ESK

Situation
Hillside, Montrose, Angus. Grampian Region

Classification
Highland (Eastern)

Origins and background
This distillery has changed its name more often than most. It was built in 1897 at the height of the whisky boom by a firm with the unlikely name of Septimus Parsonage & Co. Ltd. It was then known as the Highland Esk Distillery. It was soon acquired by a firm of distillers called Heddle and was renamed the North Esk, the source of its' water supply. Damaged by fire in 1910, it was rebuilt, but closed during the 1914-18 War. In 1919 it was acquired by Thomas Bernard & Co. and used as a maltings. In 1938 it was bought by Associated Scottish Distilleries Ltd, and turned into a patent-still grain distillery, known as the Montrose Distillery. In 1954 it was acquired by the DCL and began malt whisky distilling again in 1965, at this stage re-named Hillside. In 1980 the name was once more changed to Glenesk, then finally to Glen Esk, before the distillery was closed in 1985 and the distilling license cancelled in 1992. The whisky was mostly used for blending but was also bottled at 12 years.

Owned by
UDV

Visitors
No

Age and strength when bottled
12 years at 40% volume

Comments
A sound faintly sweetish after-dinner dram with a clean dry aftermath, but is now only available from the independent bottlers.

GLEN GARIOCH (*glen geery*)

Situation
Old Meldrum, Aberdeenshire, Grampian Region

Classification
Highland (East)

Origins and background
Founded in 1797, in the village of Old Meldrum, 20 miles n.w. of Aberdeen, the distillery was bought by J.F.Thomson & Co of Leith in 1840 and in the 1860s was acquired by Wm Sanderson & Son, Ltd., blenders of the famous 'Vat 69'. In 1937 it was taken over by DCL, but due to continual water shortages and with a working capacity of only 140,000 gallons was closed in 1968. In 1970 it was sold to Stanley P.Morrison Ltd of Glasgow, who sank a deep well nearby tapping an entirely new source of water. With peat from Pitsligo Moss and with a new wash still in 1973 it has been distilling 500,000 proof gallons annually, or 1,297,500 litres of alcohol. Waste-heat from the distillery was at one time used to heat glasshouses growing fruits and vegetables.

Owned by
Morrison Bowmore Distillers Co. ltd.

Visitors
No

Age & Strength when Bottled
8 years at 40% volume; 15 and 21 years at 43% volume

Comments
The 8 year old is a good sound dram to be recommended at any time. The 15 year old is greatly improved with age. The 21 year old is a smooth full-bodied peaty malt with a fine aftermath.

GLEN GRANT

Situation
Rothes, Morayshire. Grampian Region

Classification
Highland (Speyside)

Origins and background
There has to be something special about the professional men of Elgin and for that matter the name Grant as well, for it was an Elgin lawyer, James Grant, who in partnership with his younger brother John in 1840 founded the Glen Grant distillery on the banks of the Glen Grant burn near the village of Rothes. They had admittedly been distilling at nearby Dandaleith since 1834, so they knew what they were about and it was not long before they were enlarging their new distillery and producing 40,000 gallons a year. The introduction of the railway line, which the Grant family did much to encourage, was a great step forward from transport to the coast by horse and allowed them to expand considerably. The distillery was already a very successful concern when Major James Grant took over control on his father's death in 1872. It was he who decided to expand by building another distillery in 1897 across the road from the original one and joined by a pipe. Called initially Glen Grant No. 2 this was eventually re-named Caperdonich. (See above) The company, by this time known as J. & J. Grant, Glen Grant Ltd, merged in 1932 with George and J. G. Smith Ltd to form The Glenlivet and Glen Grant Distilleries Ltd. In 1970 they merged with Hill Thomson & Co. Ltd and Longmorn-Glenlivet Distilleries Ltd, the name of the merged company being rationalised to The Glenlivet Distillers Ltd. Finally in 1978 they were in turn taken over by Seagram Distillers plc.

Owned by
Seagram Distillers plc

Visitors
Reception Centre and Museum – On the Whisky Trail. Open April to the end of October. Tel: 01542 783318: Fax: 01542 783304

Age and strength when bottled
No age given at 40% volume, 5 years old at 40% volume and
10 years at 43% volume

Comments
Before the Seagram take-over this excellent very early maturing malt whisky used to be bottled and readily available
at 5, 10 and 15 years. Unfortunately it has become too
popular, selling over 500,000 cases of 5 year old annually
in Italy alone. It is now sometimes quite hard to find, but as a
favourite amongst the independent bottlers all is not lost.
The first noted above with no age given is a good dry dram.
The second at 5 years old is a pale coloured light and tasty
dram, which one can understand being popular in Italy or
anywhere else. The 10 year old is a medium light very dry
and satisfactory malt whisky. Some of the independent
bottlings are excellent.

GLEN ISLA *see* CAOL ISLA

GLEN KEITH

Situation
Keith, Banffshire. Grampian Region

Classification
Highland (Speyside)

Origins and background
In 1957 Seagram of Canada bought a flour mill in Keith from the Angus Milling Co. Ltd through their subsidiary Chivas Brothers, Ltd. After a year's intensive programme of re-building a new distillery was opened on the site in 1958. This was the first distillery in Scotland to use gas-fired stills in place of the traditional coal-fired stills and first to be built since the 19th century.The water for distilling is obtained from the Newmill Spring and peat comes from Knockando. Originally called the Glenkeith-Glenlivet distillery on the acquisition of The Glenlivet Distillers the affix was dropped by Seagram. Although previously it was all used for blending with only a little bottled by independent bottlers. Like UDV, Seagram have now appreciated that it is worth bottling and selling their own single malts and since 1994 Glen Keith has been generally available. It was mothballed in 1999.

Owned by
Seagram Distillers plc

Visitors
No

Age and strength when bottled
10 years at 43% volume

Comments
Although most is used for blending this addition to the generally available single malts is well worth bottling. Other distillers, who have not yet done so, should follow UDV and Seagram's example. This is a pleasant dram before or after a meal.

GLEN MORAY

Situation
Elgin, Morayshire. Grampian Region

Classification
Highland (Speyside)

Origins and background
The old road into Elgin passes through the site of this
distillery, founded in 1897. It was originally the town's West
Brewery owned by Henry Arnot & Co., obtaining its water
from the river Lossie. Unfortunately very little appears to
have been recorded of its early history until 1920 when it was
acquired by Macdonald & Muir Ltd, by which time it had
already been closed for a lengthy period. In 1958 the entire
distillery underwent a considerable amount of development
and enlargement and it now has a capacity of 700,000 gallons
a year, or 1,764,000 litres of alcohol. It has also now dropped
the Glenlivet affix on its bottlings. Although a great deal is
used for blending it is well marketed and readily available.

Owned by
Glenmorangie plc

Visitors
Reception centre. Open all year. Tel: 01343 542 577 Fax: 01343
546 195

Age and strength when bottled
Un-aged,12 and 16 years at 40% volume

Comments
An early maturing single malt, the un-aged makes a pleasing
dram. The 12 year old is a good, clean mellow all-round malt
and the 16 year old is a full-bodied satisfying after dinner
dram. This is a good sound example of a clean dry Speyside
malt.

GLEN ORD

Situation
Muir of Ord, Beauly. Highland Region

Classification
Highland (Northern)

Origins and background
The area was notorious for illicit distilling even as late as the
end of the 19th century and there is little doubt that the
distillery was built on the site of an old illicit still, but it was
only licensed in 1838. Ample water supplies are available
from Glen Oran and the Oran Burn, making illicit distilling
easy. The holder of the first license was a Mr McLennan.
When he died his widow married an Alexander McKenzie,
who thus acquired the distillery as well. It was then acquired
by John Watson & Co. Ltd, of Dundee, and finally in 1924
was bought by John Dewar just prior to their take-over by
the DCL. It is notable that heather is mixed with the peat
during the malt drying process and the taste of the malt
probably owes something to this. Although much goes for
blending it is also bottled by the distillers, but no longer
marketed under the names Ord, or Glenordie, as used to be
the case. It is now sold as Glen Ord at 12 years old.

Owned by
UDV

Visitors
Reception centre. Only closed at Christmas and New Year.
Tel: 01463 872004; Fax: 01463 872008

Age and strength when bottled
12 years old at 40% volume

Comments
A good dry and full-bodied malt whisky with a clean aftermath well worth drinking at any time.

GLEN SCOTIA

Situation
Campbeltown. Strathclyde Region

Classification
Campbeltown (West Coast)

Origins and background
The distillery was built by the Galbraith family in 1832, close to the Parliament Square in the centre of Campbeltown and was at first named the Scotia. With ample water, peat, coal and barley available locally during the 19th century it was one of the thirty-four distilleries, which provided the small town with the proud boast that it was 'the whisky capital of Scotland'. Indifferent distilling and the sale of immature whiskies gave the area a bad name with disastrous results. The Glen Scotia distillery is now one of the only two left. It was owned by A. Gillies & Co. Ltd, but was acquired by Barton International plc, who modernised the premises in the early 80s. A management buy-out in 1988 by Gibson International plc ended in receivership in 1994. Control then finally passed to the Loch Lomond Distillery Co., Ltd, who are looking for a purchaser.

Owned by
Loch Lomond Distillery Co. Ltd

Visitors
By arrangement. Tel: 01586 552288

Age and strength when bottled
14 years old at 40% volume

Comments
The Glen Scotia single malt has a rich peaty slightly oily taste with an affinity to Irish whiskey, but with a strong and interesting aftermath. Not easily found, but a good dram.

GLEN SPEY

Situation
Rothes, Morayshire. Grampian Region

Classification
Highland (Speyside)

Origins and background
Built originally in 1885 by James Stuart as the Mills of Rothes with the intention of milling cereals, but seeing whisky distilling was more profitable he converted the operation. However his heart does not seem to have been in it for in 1887 he sold out to the Gilbey brothers, Walter and Alfred, who while starting as wine merchants and progressing to gin distilling had quickly appreciated the potential of whisky distilling. Absorbed into International Distillers and Vintners Ltd in 1962, hence now part of UDV, the distillery obtains its water from the Doonie burn and has a capacity of 750,000 proof gallons, almost all of which goes for blending, although some no doubt forms part of the vatted malt Strathspey marketed by the parent company. It used to add the Glenlivet affix, but this has now been dropped. Currently none is bottled.

Owned by
UDV

Visitors
Only by arrangement

Age and strength when bottled
8 years at 40% volume

Comments
This is very clearly a Speyside malt whisky, making a pleasant and very smooth pre-prandial dram.

GLENALLACHIE

Situation
Aberlour, Banffshire. Grampian Region

Classification
Highland (Speyside)

Origins and background
Built in the mini-boom years of the 1960s under Ben Rinnes from where it obtains its' water. Mr Delme Evans, the architect. designed two more distilleries, one on the Isle of Jura above Islay and the other at Tullibardine in Perthshire. Glenallachie and Isle of Jura were both then owned by Scottish and Newcastle Breweries Ltd, who had obviously liked his work on their Isle of Jura distillery in 1958. Both were acquired in 1985 by Invergordon Distillers and Glenallachie was temporarily closed. It was acquired in 1989 by Pernod Ricard through their subsidiary Campbell Distillers Ltd and re-opened.

Owned by
Campbell Distillers Ltd.

Visitors
By arrangement

Age and strength when bottled
None bottled

Comments
A 12 year old independent bottling was a smooth light dram with a subtle fragrance in the aftermath well worth bottling.

GLENBURGIE

Situation
Forres, Morayshire. Grampian Region

Classification
Highland (Speyside)

Origins and background
Another distillery which can claim to be among the oldest in the Highlands as it is said to have been established in 1810 by William Paul with a modest capacity of 90 gallons. It changed hands a number of times during the 19th century and each change of ownership appears to have resulted in an increase in its capacity so that when it was taken over by Alexander Fraser & Co. in the 1890s the wash still had a capacity of 1,500 gallons. The distillery was subsequently acquired by James & George Stodart Ltd of Dumbarton, who were themselves taken over by Hiram Walker (Scotland) Ltd, in 1930, in their first venture into the Scotch Whisky industry. Two spirit stills and two wash-stills were added in 1958, but removed in 1980. For a while the whisky produced from them was known as Glencraig. The malt whisky is no longer marketed as Glenburgie-Glenlivet, although the affix is still sometimes used.

Owned by
Allied Distillers

Visitors
By arrangement. Tel: 01343 850258

Age and strength when bottled
Only at present bottled by the independent bottlers.

Comments
This a fairly typical light Speyside malt whisky and as such a good dram, which deserves to be more widely available Although twenty miles from Glenlivet the firm still seems ambivalent about using the Glenlivet affix.

GLENCADAM

Situation
Brechin, Angus. Tayside Region

Classification
Highland (Eastern)

Origins and background
Situated in a steep-sided glen the distillery obtains ample water supplies from the Moorfoot Loch. It was first licensed in 1825 and as with many around this date was almost certainly built on the site of a previously illicit still. It went through a number of changes of ownership until acquired in 1891 by Gilmour Thomson & Co. Ltd. The distillery was finally bought by Hiram Walker and Sons (Scotland) Ltd in 1954, as another acquisition in their then expanding empire. The whisky all goes for blending, but is obtainable from the independent bottlers. Currently mothballed.

Owned by
Allied Distillers

Visitors
No

Age and strength when bottled
A 15 year old at 46% volume is available from Miltonduff

Comments
A good clean after-dinner malt worth while making more widely available.

GLENDRONACH

Situation
Forgue, by Huntly, Aberdeenshire. Grampian Region

Classification
Highland (Speyside)

Origins and background
The distillery was built in 1826 by James Allardyce and a syndicate of local businessmen. Unfortunately mismanagement and financial losses in the early years were followed by an extensive fire in 1837 after which the distillery was taken over by Mr Walter Scott. Its history thereafter was fairly straightforward. It takes its name and water from the Dronach burn. It was acquired by Captain Charles Grant, one of the Grants of the Glenfiddich distilling family, until sold to William Teacher & Sons Ltd in 1960. It retained certain old-fashioned features such as floor maltings and coal-fired potstills, but was extensively modernised and enlarged from two to four stills in 1967. Until then it had used the hyphenated Glenlivet prefix, but this was dropped. Local control is in the hands of the Glendronach Distillery Company Limited, Huntly, and comparatively recently production doubled but it is now mothballed

Owned by
Allied Distillers

Visitors
Reception centre. Tel: 01466 730202 Fax: 01466 730243

Age and strength when bottled
12 years at 40% volume

Comments
Comes as The Traditional,(previously The Original) aged in oak and sherry wood casks and much favoured in Aberdeenshire. A touch peppery initially, but a very good after-dinner dram with a distinctive long dry aftermath.

GLENDULLAN

Situation
Dufftown, Banffshire. Grampian Region

Classification
Highland (Speyside)

Origins and background
The distillery, the seventh around Dufftown, was built in 1896 by William Williams & Sons Ltd of Aberdeen, whisky blenders and merchants who used most of the malt whisky produced for their blends, although some was bottled as a single malt of sufficient distinction to acquire a Royal Warrant in 1902 as supplied to King Edward VII. Their water comes from springs in the Conval hills During the 1914-18 War they merged with Macdonald Greenlees and formed Macdonald Greenlees and Williams (Distillers) Ltd, being subsequently acquired by the DCL. In 1971 a new distillery with six stills was built near the old distillery, which closed in 1985.

Owned by
UDV

Visitors
No

Age and strength when bottled
12 years at 43% volume

Comments
A smooth dram with a good aftermath this makes a good after-dinner Speyside malt whisky which deserves to be better known.

GLENFARCLAS

Situation
Marypark, Ballindalloch, Banffshire. Grampian Region

Classification
Highland (Speyside)

Origins and background
Possibly mentioned in the 1791 Statistical Account but first
licensed in 1836, the distillery obtains its' water from springs
on Ben Rinnes. Purchased in 1865 by John Grant, by which
time the affix Glenlivet had been added to the Glenfarclas
name, it was initially sub-let to John Smith, at the nearby
Glenlivet Distillery. John Grant took over control of the
distillery in 1870, handing over increasingly to his son
George before his death in 1889. Unfortunately George then
died prematurely in 1890 but his wife managed the business
successfully until their sons, John and George, were old
enough to take over in 1895. In that year they formed The
Glenfarclas-Glenlivet Distillery Co. Ltd, on an equal share
basis with the Leith blenders Pattison, Elder & Co. In 1896 at
the height of the whisky boom they instituted rebuilding and
renovations which brought the production up to nearly
300,000 proof gallons a year, or 778,500 litres of alcohol.
In 1898 the Pattison brothers bankruptcy signalled the end of
the whisky boom and thereafter the Grant brothers remained
in full control. John Grant retired from the partnership after
the 1914-18 War, but George remained in sole charge until
1947 when he formed J.& G. Grant, a private company. On
his death in 1949 control passed to the family and his sons
George Scott Grant, then appointed Chairman, and John P.
Grant. The latter died in 1960, but George Grant remains
Chairman (for a record 51 years) with his son John, as M/D
and his grandson, George, the sixth generation, in the firm.
Without the affix Glenlivet, Glenfarclas has now for generations proudly distilled under its' own name. It is, however,
indicative of the long depression in the industry that it was
not until 1960 that considerable rebuilding and modernisation doubled the capacity from two to four stills producing

600,000 gallons, or 1,557,000 litres of alcohol. In 1976 with two more stills added the annual capacity was raised yet again to a million gallons, or 2.595 million litres of alcohol.

Owned by
J. & G. Grant

Visitors
Reception Centre - On the Whisky Trail. Open all year: Tel: 01807 500 245 or 257: Fax: 01807 500 234:

Age and strength when bottled*
10 years at 40% volume; 12 years at 43% volume (export only): 15 years at 46% volume; 21, 25 and 30 years at 43% volume:
Original cask strength at 60% volume;

Comments
With over 130 years of the same family in control this must be unique even in an industry where tradition and continuity counts for a great deal. This is a malt whisky of character and Glenfarclas is a fine dram at any time and any age and strength.

GLENFIDDICH

Situation
Dufftown, Banffshire. Grampian Region

Classification
Highland (Speyside)

Origins and background
The founding of this distillery, like that of Glenfarclas, is very much a family story relating yet again to the name Grant, itself amongst the most notable and frequently found wherever Scotch whisky is distilled. Although starting some twenty years after the Grants of Glenfarclas the Grants of Glenfiddich made up for matters by sheer numbers. In 1886 William Grant who already had twenty years experience of distilling in the Mortlach distillery bought the land on the Robbie Dhu springs nearby. He also bought the old disused plant from the Cardow distillery which was then being re-equipped for £120 and set about building his own distillery, using water for cooling purposes from the nearby Fiddich burn from which the distillery gained its name of Glenfiddich. With the aid of his seven sons and his entire capital of £755 he had the distillery producing whisky by 1887 and was so successful that in five years he was building Balvenie close at hand. Thereafter expansion was steady with the formation of a limited company William Grant & Sons Ltd in 1903 with which William Grant remained actively involved until his death in 1923. Meanwhile Captain Charles Grant one of his sons had taken over the Glendronach distillery (sold to William Teacher in 1960, see Glendronach) and in the post 1939-45 boom years the firm, still very much a family concern, built a grain distillery at Girvan in Ayrshire, near which they built a Lowland malt distillery named Ladyburn used entirely for blending and now closed. The success of their blend Grant's Standfast, which owed much to skilful marketing was followed in the 1960s by the widespread foreign sales and marketing of the Glenfiddich, the first determinedly successful overseas sales of a malt whisky, gaining a Queen's Award to Industry for Export Achieve-

ment in 1974. Still very much a family company William Grant & Sons Ltd continue to manage Glenfiddich and the neighbouring Balvenie distilleries as well as the Girvan plant and their worldwide blending and marketing projects with determination and flair, while Grants are still prominent in the board of directors, the grandsons and great grandsons of William and his progeny. It is a remarkable success story by any standards.

Owned by
William Grant & Sons Ltd

Visitors
Reception centre – On the Whisky Trail. Open all year: Tel: 01340 820373 Fax: 01340 822083

Age and strength when bottled*
12 years at 40% volume: 18, 21 and 30 years at 40% volume. 15 years Solera Reserve at 40% volume.

Comments
With widespread overseas sales and the many distillery visitors the 12 year old must be amongst the malt whiskies most frequently drunk for the first time. It is a good clean introduction to single malts which should interest and encourage those who have not drunk any previously, mellowing richly with age. The Solera Reserve is vatted in sherry, bourbon and new wood casks before finishing in a Solera vat and bottling. A complex dram.

GLENGLASSAUGH

Situation
Portsoy, Banffshire. Grampian Region

Classification
Highland (Speyside)

Origins and background
This distillery was built in 1875 about a couple of miles along the coast from the small fishing village of Portsoy, six and a half miles west of Banff itself. It obtains its water from the Glassaugh spring close to the site. The Highland Distillers acquired it in 1892. Completely rebuilt and renovated in 1959 with two stills and an output of 1.2 million litres of alcohol, most went for blending, although some was bottled by the distillery and the independent bottlers. Currently closed, the distillery became part of the Edrington Group when they acquired Highland Distillers in 1999.

Owned by
Highland Distillers Ltd.

Visitors
No.

Age and strength when bottled
Only obtainable through independent bottlings.

Comments
To judge by one 13 year old bottling this is a pleasant slightly sweetish dram with a dry aftermath which deserves to be more easily available.

GLENGOYNE

Situation
Dumgoyne, Stirlingshire (2 miles S.E. of Killearn). Tayside Region

Classification
Highland (South West)

Origins and background
Sited in a wooded glen at the foot of Dumgoyne Hill, the water supply comes from the nearby Campsie Fells. This is a particularly attractively placed small distillery and is a very suitable one for visitors who want to see the whole process without too much walking. It is also very convenient for Glasgow. First licensed to Archibald McLellan in 1833 it was then known as the Glenguin distillery. When it was taken over by the brothers Alexander and Gavin Lang in 1876 it was re-named the Glengoyne distillery. In 1965 Lang Brothers Ltd were taken over by Robertson & Baxter Ltd, part of the Edrington Group, and the distillery was then completely modernised. It is a very good example of a well-run small Scottish-owned distillery.

Owned by
Robertson & Baxter Ltd.

Visitors
Restaurant and Reception centre open all year including weekends. Tel: 01360 550 254: Fax:

Age and strength when bottled
10 years at 40% volume; 12 and 17 years at 43% volume

Comments
Situated right on the imaginary Highland Line it may be classified as a Southern Highland malt whisky, but regardless of position the 10 year old is a light, clean and pleasant dram. The 12 year old is rather more mature and smoother and the 17 year old even more so. It thus, like many malt whiskies, changes with age from a good pre-dinner dram to a good after-dinner dram.

GLENKINCHIE

Situation
Glenkinchie, Pencaitland, East Lothian. Lothian Region

Classification
Lowland (East)

Origins and background
Built around 1837 by local farmers John and George Rate, the distillery was subsequently sold to another East Lothian farmer named Christie, who bought it not for distilling, but for use as a sawmill and cattle shed. In 1880 it was sold again to a syndicate interested in turning it back into a distillery. In 1890, as the whisky boom developed, they formed the Glenkinchie Distillery Company. In 1914 it was taken over by the Scottish Malt Distillers Ltd, since when it has been considerably modernised and rebuilt, but still using water from the nearby Lammermuir hills, which rises from a spring within the distillery, as well as the excellent local barley. Most of the whisky still goes for blending, but when control passed to United Distillers it also became readily available as a single malt whisky.

Owned by
UDV

Visitors
Reception centre and museum. Tel: 01875 342004. Fax: 01875 342007: Popular as the nearest to Edinburgh. Open all year;

Age and strength when bottled***
10 years old and 43% volume.

Comments
There is an attractive dryness about this distinctively Lowland malt whisky, making a good clean dram with a smooth aftermath. With the demise of Kinclaith and Ladyburn, and Bladnoch on part-time (see above) this is the most southern fully operative Lowland distillery and happily the 10 year old single malt is widely available as another of UDV's six 'Classic Malts'.

THE GLENLIVET

Situation
Minmore, Banffshire. Grampian Region

Classification
Highland (Speyside)

Origins and background
Thomas Smith, great grandfather of the George Smith who founded The Glenlivet Distillery in 1824 in what was still then wild and desolate part of the Highlands, was probably out with his laird in the 1715 Rebellion, supporting the Jacobites, but he does not seem to have supported them in the 1745 Rising. It may have been because of this that he and his family appear to have escaped any of the draconian punishments imposed by the Duke of Cumberland after the '45.

In 1817, when Thomas' great grandson, George Smith, took over from his father Andrew at Upper Drumin as one of the Duke of Gordon's tenants, illicitly made 'Glenlivet' whisky was known and popular as far south as Edinburgh. With the Duke's encouragement and backing George was the first to take out a license in 1824 under the Act of 1823 and start distilling legally despite fierce opposition from his erstwhile friends, who still continued to distil illicitly. It was thus in 1824 that the distillery at Upper Drumin was amongst the first to distil legally, with a capacity of fifty gallons weekly which by 1839 had risen dramatically four times to 200 gallons a week. With his son-in-law Captain William Grant distilling at nearby Auchorachan, George Smith maintained that only they could distil whisky with the title Glenlivet.

By 1858 George and his son John Gordon Smith had built a much larger distillery at Minmore and closed down both Delnabo and Upper Drumin. The new distillery had a capacity of 600 gallons a week and as a result of the energy of their agent Andrew Usher the production was soon heavily in demand and by 1864 being exported abroad. In 1871 John Gordon Smith inherited the distillery on his father's death. In 1884 he established by due process of law that no-one else was legally entitled to the use of the name The Glenlivet, but all others must use a prefix. John Gordon Smith was succeeded in 1901 by his nephew George Smith Grant, son of Captain William Grant of Ruthven.

In 1921 the distillery went to Captain W. H. Smith Grant his younger son. In 1952 George and J. G. Smith Ltd merged with J. & J. Grant, Glen Grant Distillery forming the Glenlivet and Glen Grant Distilleries Ltd. In 1970 they merged yet again with the noted blenders Hill Thomson & Co. Ltd and Longmorn-Glenlivet Distilleries Ltd when the name of the merged companies was rationalised to The Glenlivet Distillers Ltd. In 1978 their long record of independence came to an end with their acquisition by Seagram Distillers plc.

Owned by
Seagram Distillers plc

Visitors
Reception centre. April to October inclusive:Tel: 01542 783220

Age and strength when bottled***
12 years at 40% volume 18 years at 43% volume; 21 years at 43% volume.

Comments
Although still an excellent and outstanding malt whisky there is perhaps a suspicion of a blander style becoming more apparent than in the past in the 12 year old. However, the 18 year old is a decidedly smooth and full bodied dram by any standards and the 21 year old is a very satisfying after dinner dram.

GLENLOSSIE

Situation
Elgin, Morayshire. Grampian Region

Classification
Highland (Speyside)

Origins and background
Built in 1876 at Thomshill, about two and a half miles south of Elgin by a partnership formed by a local hotel owner John Duff, who had been manager of Glendronach distillery. In 1896 the partnership was dissolved and The Glenlossie-Glenlivet Distillery Co. Ltd., was formed. In 1897 after considerable development including a private railway line to Longmorn Station and a new warehouse the company went public. The recession in the Scotch Whisky industry during the ensuing years, however, resulted in the Scottish Malt Distillers Ltd taking them over in 1919 and in 1930 the company was dissolved. In 1971 the Mannochmore distillery was built nearby on the same site, both taking their water from the Bardon burn. The bulk of production still goes for blending, but some is now available.

Owned by
UDV

Visitors
No

Age and strength when bottled
10 years at 43% volume

Comments
Although not widely available this does seem to make a pleasant dram well worth bottling and a welcome addition to the available single malts.

GLENMORANGIE (*glen morange-y*)

Situation
Tain, Ross-shire. Highland Region

Classification
Highland (Northern)

Origins and background
Above the Dornoch Firth near the town of Tain, on a site where brewing and distilling has been carried on since the Middle Ages. The distillery, however, only dates from 1843 when William Matheson and his brother converted the brewery operating there. Its name derives from the Morangie burn which runs through a small glen beside it. It obtains its water from a spring rich in minerals from which the brewers who preceded them had taken water for their ale then renowned as far south as Inverness. In 1893 it was connected to the main railway line improving the transport of whisky to the south and making it easier to obtain supplies of local peat until these were exhausted. The use of steam coils in the stills to separate the alcohol from the wash to avoid affecting the whisky's flavour was initiated here and subsequently copied by a number of others in the Highlands. In 1918 it was acquired by Macdonald & Muir Ltd, now Glenmorangie plc., and now produces about 600,000 gallons a year, mostly bottled at 10 years.

Owned by
Glenmorangie plc

Visitors
Reception centre. Tel: 01862 892043

Age and strength when bottled
10 years at 40% and 18 years at 43% volume.

Comments
The 10 year old makes a full-bodied pre-dinner dram. The 16 year old is mellower to be drunk with pleasure after a meal. Both well known, well marketed and popular drams. There are also cask changes with interesting madeira, sherry or port finish.

GLENORDIE or ORD *see* GLEN ORD

GLENROTHES

Situation
Rothes, Morayshire. Grampian Region

Classification
Highland (Speyside)

Origins and background
The distillery was built on the site of an old sawmill in 1878 by a syndicate of Rothes and Elgin businessmen. It went into production in 1879 and eight years later in 1887 merged with the Islay Distillery Co. to form the Highland Distillers. Ltd. Since then there has been periodic extensive renovation and re-building. In 1980 a new still-house with two new pairs of stills was added, making ten in all with a capacity overall of around 5.3 million litres of spirit. Although much still goes for blending this is now also bottled at 12 and 15 years old and is found in various outlets. Acquired by the Edrington Group in 1999.

Owned by
Highland Distillers Ltd.

Visitors
Reception centre. Tel: 01340 872152

Age and strength when bottled
12 and 15 years old at 43%

Comments
The 12 year old is a good smooth dram with a pleasing aftermath . The 15 year old, interestingly different after only three years, is sold in a round bottle as Glenrothes Vintage.

GLENTAUCHERS

Situation
Mulben, Banffshire. Grampian Region

Classification
Highland (Speyside)

Origins and background
This distillery was built by James Buchanan, promoter of the famed 'Black and White' blend and prominent amongst the 'Big Five' of the late 19th century whisky boom. Although primarily a skilful salesman and promoter of blended whiskies he naturally became involved in the power struggle between the grain whisky and the pot-still malt whisky distillers. However he decided in 1898 that he needed his own supplies of malt whisky and built this distillery at Glentauchers in association with his Glaswegian whisky broker W. P. Lowrie. The controlling company was named the Glentauchers-Glenlivet Distillery Co. Ltd, which in 1906, on W. P. Lowrie's retirement, was taken over by James Buchanan & Co. Ltd. In 1925 the distillery became part of DCL. It was closed in 1985, but after its acquisition by Allied Distillers in 1989 re-opened. Mostly used for blending the malt whisky was available at 5 and 12 years, as well as through independent bottlings. Now a 15 year old is available from the Miltonduff distillery.

Owned by
Allied Distillers

Visitors
By arrangement

Age and strength when bottled
15 years at 46% volume available from Miltonduff

Comments
This seems a clean smooth Speyside malt with a slightly peaty aftermath making a pleasant dram which deserves to be more widely available

GLENTURRET

Situation
Crieff, Perthshire. Highland Region

Classification
Highland (South)

Origins and background
Built in 1775 when illicit distilling was widespread and well placed between two hills on the banks of the Turret water providing a good water supply. Glenturret claims to be the oldest distillery in Scotland. Amongst its' early proprietors, was Crieff landowner, Thomas Stewart. In 1959 James Fairlie took over and began renovation and rebuilding. Although it has a capacity of only around 400,000 litres, the distillery won Gold Medals in the International Wine and Spirit Competitions in 1974, in 1981 and again in 1991, under James Fairlie's son Peter and with third generation Stillman, Charlie Brock. In 1981 it was taken over by Cointreau SA, the French liqueur makers, and in 1990 acquired by Highland Distillers Ltd. Close to Perth, and the most visited Scottish distillery, it came under control of the Scots-owned Edrington Group in 1999. It is a very good example of a small distillery well geared to tourism.

Owned by
Highland Distillers Ltd.

Visitors
Restaurant and Reception centre. Open all year: Tel: 01764 656565 Fax: 01764 654 366

Age and strength when bottled
12, 15, 18 and 21 years at 40% volume

Comments
This is an unusually late maturing, but very sound malt whisky with a full smooth flavour and good aftermath suitable for an after-dinner dram. The later years should be drunk with respect.

HAZELBURN *see* SPRINGBANK

HIGHLAND PARK

Situation
Kirkwall, Orkney

Classification
Island (Orkney)

Origins and background
Built on a hill overlooking Kirkwall an illicit distiller named Magnus Eunson who started distilling there in the eighteenth century. He took advantage of his position as a church officer to evade capture of his illicit whisky by hiding it under the pulpit. The early history of the distillery is vague, but it is said to have been started legally by David Robertson around 1789. In 1888 James Grant, whose father had been the chief distiller and manager of the Glenlivet Distillery, became managing partner and in 1895 he acquired full control. The Grant family retained control until 1937 when the distillery was acquired by Highland Distillers Ltd. The distillery has its own maltings although barley has to be imported from the mainland. The water supply comes from two local wells. The Orkney peat has a distinctive aroma and a small quantity of heather is burnt with it that may account for the distinctive flavour of this very fine malt whisky from the northernmost distillery in Scotland. Another prize acquired by the Edrington Group in 1999.

Owned by
Highland Distillers Co., plc.

Visitors
Reception centre. Open all year: Limited winter opening: Tel: 01856 874619 Fax: 01856 8786091

Age and strength when bottled
12 and 18 years at 40% volume. 25 years at 43% volume.

Comments
This has to be acknowledged as one of the finest after-dinner drams. Smooth and full of character with a fine aftermath, the distinctively shaped bottle is always a welcome sight at any age

IMPERIAL

Situation
Carron, Morayshire. Grampian Region

Classification
Highland (Speyside)

Origins and background
The distillery was established in 1887 by Thomas Mackenzie, who already owned Dailuaine and the Talisker Distilleries. He incorporated all three distilleries in 1898 as the Dailuaine-Talisker Distilleries Ltd. In 1916 the company was acquired jointly by Dewar, DCL, W. P. Lowrie and Johnnie Walker, thus ending up as part of the DCL in 1925, the year of the great mergers into DCL. The product all went for blending except for some bottled independently. Acquired in 1989 by Allied Distillers Ltd. and closed in 1998/

Owned by
Allied Distillers

Visitors
No

Age and strength when bottled
15 years at 46% available through the Miltonduff distillery

Comments
This seems to be another fairly typical smooth Speyside malt with long peaty aftermath well worth bottling.

INCHGOWER

Situation
Buckie, Banffshire. Grampian Region

Classification
Highland (Speyside)

Origins and background
Originally established in 1824 as Tochineal Distillery close to
Cullen by Alexander Wilson, the distillery was moved in
1871 by Alexander Wilson & Co. to Rathven, a small village
about one and a half miles east of Buckie to ensure a ready
supply of water from the Letter Burn and the springs at
Aultmoor. In 1933 it was acquired and run by Buckie Town
Council, but its period of municipal ownership ended when
it was acquired by A. K. Bell in 1936 on behalf of Arthur Bell
& Sons, later themselves acquired by Guinness plc,
and merged with DCL as part of United Distillers plc.

Owned by
UDV

Visitors
No

Age and strength when bottled
14 years at 43% volume

Comments
A medium light malt with a touch of sweetness making a
pleasant distinctive dram.

INCHMURRIN *see* LOCH LOMOND

INVERLEVEN

Situation
Dumbarton, Strathclyde. Strathclyde Region

Classification
Lowland (Northern)

Origins and background
Established in 1938 adjacent to the Hiram Walker Dumbarton Grain distillery. Although situated right on the imaginary 'Highland Line', it was classified as a Lowland malt. It obtained its water from the River Leven and Loch Lomond. The production of the two main stills was used almost entirely for blending, but a unique flat-sided still, known as a Lomond still invented by a Mr Fred Whiting, using the same low wines and feints charger and same spirit receiver as Inverleven was used to produce a quite distinct heavier malt whisky known as Lomond. The whole whisky complex was acquired by Allied Distillers in 1988. In 1992 Inverleven was closed and both stills along with the Lomond still were dismantled.

Owned by
Allied Distillers

Visitors
No

Age and strength when bottled
Only obtainable through the independent bottlers

Comments
Although it could really just as well be classified as western highland this tastes more like a Lowland malt whisky. It is a light and slightly sweet dram with a dry aftermath and is unlikely to be available much longer.

ISLE OF ARRAN

Situation
Lochranza, in the north of the Isle of Arran

Classification
Island (Arran)

Origins and background
Harold Currie previously managing director of Chivas Brothers was one of the prime movers in raising £2.5 million to build this distillery on Arran beside the village of Lochranza on the northern tip of the Island. Although much illicit distilling took place in the 18th century as elsewhere in Scotland this is the first legal distillery on the island. The water used comes from the Eason Biorach burn rising in the mountains. The distillery has two stills with a capacity of 500,000 litres. It came on stream in 1995 and the first malt was sampled in 1999 after four years and proved to be a very early maturing single malt already quite drinkable and likely to be a good mature dram at eight years.

Owned by
Isle of Arran Distillers Ltd.

Visitors
Reception Centre: Open April to October. Tel: 01770 830264
Fax: 01770 830364

+Age and strength when bottled
Un-aged and 8 years at 43% volume

Comments
From an un-aged sample this is an early maturing single malt. Somewhat light at this age and possibly more reminiscent of a Lowland than an island malt, when more mature it should make a very good dram with a distinctive peaty touch.

ISLE OF JURA

Situation
Craighouse, Isle of Jura, Argyll. Strathclyde Region

Classification
Island (Jura)

Origins and background
It is said there was distilling at Craighouse as early as the seventeenth century, but the present distillery only dates from around 1810. The buildings were owned by the Campbells, landlords of the Jura estate, but the stills and equipment belonged to James Ferguson who operated the distillery for his own profit. This arrangement ceased in 1901 when the parties to it quarrelled. Ferguson removed his equipment and the landlords removed the roof to avoid the payment of rates. In 1958 Mr Riley-Smith and Mr Fletcher, two island landowners, put a proposal to Scottish and Newcastle Breweries to rebuild the distillery to bring fresh employment to Jura. The distillery was built by Charles Mackinlay & Co. Ltd, a subsidiary of Scottish & Newcastle Breweries Ltd, to the design of Mr Delme Morgan and went into production in 1963 under the name of the Isle of Jura Distillery Co. Ltd. It was later acquired by Invergordon Distillers Ltd, taken over in 1994 by Whyte & Mackay and now part of Jim Beam Brands(Greater Europe) plc.

Owned by
JBB (Greater Europe) plc

Visitors
Reception centre. Tel: 01496 820240

Age and strength when bottled*
10, 16 and 21 years at 40% volume

Comments
Although just north of Islay this much more resembles a Highland malt whisky than an Islay malt. It is a pleasant smooth, light bodied and clean tasting dram improving with age.

KININVIE

Situation
Dufftown, Banffshire, Grampian Region

Classification
Highland (Speyside)

Origins and background
Another distillery to add to the two already built over the years by William Grant & Sons at Dufftown. The Kininvie Distillery is named after the nearby Kininvie Estate and is situated about five hundred yards from the well-known Glenfiddich distillery. This modern plant was planned in the 1980s and takes its water from the Robbie Dhu springs. It came on-stream in July 1990 and has three wash stills with a capacity of 14,700 litres and six spirit stills with a capacity of 8,400 litres, rather larger than Glenfiddich itself.

Owned by
William Grant & Sons, Ltd

Visitors
No

Age & Strength when bottled
None as yet bottled

Comments
So far it is only used for blending and none is bottled as a single malt, but if it is ever available it will be interesting to compare it with Glenfiddich since both distilleries obtain their water from nearly the same source, the Robbie Dhu springs.

KNOCKANDO

Situation
Knockando, Morayshire. Grampian Region

Classification
Highland (Speyside)

Origins and background
The distillery was built by Ian Thompson at the end of the whisky boom and only went into small scale production for a couple of years before closing down and falling into disrepair but in 1904 it was bought cheaply by W. & A. Gilbey. The Gaelic meaning of the name is 'black hill' and it is in a good position above the Spey with a good water supply. The distillery has a capacity of 750,000 gallons and became part of International Distillers & Vintners. While most of the production then went into the well known J & B Rare Blend, it was the best known of the IDV malt whiskies, but now, of course, as part of UDV, it may be subject to rationalisation.

Owned by
UDV

Visitors
No. By arrangement only. Tel: 01340 810205

Age and strength when bottled
Generally from around 13 to 15 years at 40% and 43% volume

Comments
This is a light and smooth after-dinner dram with a good distinctive aftermath. It is a pleasing Speyside malt whisky, bottled when considered at its best by the distillery manager. The dates of distilling and bottling are on the label.

KNOCKDHU (nokdoo)

Situation
Knock, Banffshire. Grampian Region

Classification
Highland (Speyside)

Origins and background
Knockdhu stands between the small river Isla and the Deveron but draws its water from a spring on the Knock hill. Built in 1894 and of historic interest as the first malt whisky distillery to be built by the DCL. All its production was used for blending, but some was occasionally available from the independent bottlers. The distillery was closed in 1983 during the recession in the industry, but it was acquired in 1988 by Inver House Distillers Ltd, the first acquisition by this rapidly developing Scottish group, and distilling promptly re-started in 1989. It is sold under the name An Cnoc, the Gaelic for Knockdhu, to avoid confusion with Knockando.

Owned by
Inver House Distillers Ltd

Visitors
By appointment only

Age and strength when bottled
12 years at 40% volume

Comments
This is a medium dry typically sound Speyside after-dinner dram with a pleasing aftermath.

LAGAVULIN (lag-avoolin)

Situation
Port Ellen, on the south of the Isle of Islay, Argyll. Strathclyde Region

Classification
Islay (Island West Coast)

Origins and background
The Gaelic meaning of Lagavulin is 'the mill in the valley' and it claims to date back to 1742, but the modern distillery was probably built nearer 1824. It is close beside the village of Lagavulin in a small bay with its own jetty and obtains its water from the lochs in the hill of Solan. There were a number of owners in the 19th century, latterly James Logan Mackie, uncle of the famous Peter prominent amongst the 'Big Five' in the late 19th century. It was here that Peter Mackie trained as a distiller and on his uncle's death in the late 1880s he inherited the distillery. The whisky was used as the basis for his famous 'White Horse' blend on which his subsequent reputation was founded. When DCL took over Mackie & Co., Distillers, Ltd., after his death in 1927 they changed the name to White Horse Distillers Ltd, one of the few examples of a company being named after a blend rather than vice-versa. The bulk goes for blending but it is now readily available.

Owned by
UDV

Visitors
Reception centre. All year. Tel 01496 302400: Fax 01496 302733

Age and strength when bottled***
16 years at 43% volume

Comments
A full-bodied malt whisky with a powerful iodine flavour and aftermath it has all the distinctive southern Islay character. Considered by many to be the most distinctive of the Islay malt whiskies it has a notable smoothness making a memorable dram. Another of the 'Classic Malts'.

LAPHROAIG (*la-froig*)

Situation
Port Ellen, on the south of the Isle of Islay, Argyll. Strathclyde Region

Classification
Islay (Island West Coast)

Origins and background
About one mile from Port Ellen this distillery is in a most attractive position set on a small bay protected by rocky islets. Built around 1820, illicitly, by two brothers, Donald and Alexander Johnston. Donald took over sole control in 1836, by which time the distillery was licensed. Ownership passed through the family until in 1928 Ian Hunter became sole owner. In 1950 he formed D. Johnston & Co. Ltd with a Miss E. L. Williamson (later Mrs Campbell) as Secretary and Director. On his death in 1954 she took over as Managing Director. When the company was acquired by Long John International Ltd, acting for Seager Evans & Co. in 1967 she continued as Chairman and Director until her death in 1972, a rare example of a female in charge of what is largely a male preserve. Acquired in 1990 by Allied Distillers Ltd. and one of their best known malts.

Owned by
Allied Distillers

Visitors
Welcome by appointment. Tel: 01496 302418 Fax: 01496 302496

Age and strength when bottled
10 and 15 years at 40% volume

Comments
A very distinctively southern Islay dram, slightly sweeter and not as full bodied as Lagavulin, but with a definite character of its' own. The 15 year old is drier and more full bodied, but at either age, like Lagavulin this is a malt whisky about which strong views are held both for and against.

LEDAIG (ledaish) *see* TOBERMORY

LINKWOOD

Situation
Elgin, Morayshire. Grampian Region

Classification
Highland (Speyside)

Origins and background
Standing just a mile outside Elgin in wooded surroundings this distillery was originally established by Peter Brown in 1821. It was named after the old mansion house which it replaced. The distillery was largely rebuilt by his son William Brown in 1873. Control was passed to the Linkwood-Glenlivet Distillery Ltd, in 1896. For thirty years from 1902 until 1932 the company was managed by a Mr Innes Cameron, who established its reputation as producing a sound malt whisky. On his death the distillery was acquired by the DCL. It is still produced as a malt whisky, although much goes for blending.

Owned by
UDV

Visitors
No

Age and strength when bottled
12 years at 40% volume

Comments
A very much under-rated malt whisky this is a very good, slightly peaty and very clean tasting Speyside dram with a good aftermath well worth drinking at any time.

LITTLEMILL

Situation
Bowling, Dunbartonshire. Strathclyde Region

Classification
Lowland (Western)

Origins and background
Possibly amongst the oldest distilleries in Scotland, it may date back as far as 1750 when Glasgow maltster, George Buchanan, purchased the estate of Auchterlonie, including Littlemill. Distilling probably started around 1800. After numerous owners a U.S. citizen, Duncan G. Thomas,, took it over in 1931 and formed the Littlemill Distillery Co. Ltd. In 1959 Barton Brands Inc. of Chicago became shareholders and in 1971 bought out D. G. Thomas and took control forming Barton Distilling (Scotland) Ltd. After a management buy-out in 1988 Barton International became Gibson International and control finally passed to the Loch Lomond Distillery Co., Ltd. Since it used highland peat and water from the Kilpatrick hills this might have been regarded as a borderline case, but it was rightly classified as Lowland. Most of the whisky was used for blending, but some was bottled by the distillery. In 1996 most of the plant was dismantled and became part of a housing scheme. The remaining warehouse is for sale and although a modified plant could still be installed there, it too may go for housing.

Owned by
Loch Lomond Distillery Co. Ltd.

Visitors
No.

Age and strength when bottled
8 years at 40% volume

Comments
A light and rather pleasing smooth pre-dinner dram. It is not likely to be available for very much longer.

LOCH LOMOND

Situation
Alexandria. Strathclyde Region

Classification
Highland (South Western)

Origins and background
Located at Alexandria, close to Loch Lomond, from which it takes its name, the distillery was built on the site of an old printing and bleach works. It was also built almost exactly on the imaginary 'Highland Line' and just qualifies as producing a Highland malt whisky. The stills are unusual in that incorporated with them is a rectifying head, which can be altered to produce different weights of whisky. The bulk of the malt whisky produced goes for blending. After the take-over of Barton Distilling (Scotland) Ltd, by Amalgamated Distilled Products plc in 1982, control passed to the Loch Lomond Distillery Co., Ltd. Some malt whisky is now distilled and bottled under the name Inchmurrin after a prominent island on nearby Loch Lomond. Using the rectifying head on the same stills, a separate malt whisky named Old Rosdhu, after a sandbank above the island, is also distilled. A grain distillery has been added.

Owned by
Loch Lomond Distillery Co. Ltd

Visitors
By arrangement

Age and strength when bottled
Inchmurrin at 10 years at 40% volume. Old Rosdhu unaged at 43% volume

Comments
Somewhat hard to find, Inchmurrin is an interesting if rather light single malt. Old Rosdhu seems heavier, with a drier aftermath, but the age gap makes judging difficult.

LOCHNAGER *see* ROYAL LOCHNAGAR

LOCHSIDE

Situation
Lochside, Montrose, Angus. Grampian Region

Classification
Highland (Eastern)

Origins and background
Built in the 18th century as a brewery, in the early 19th century it was sold to James Deuchar & Sons Ltd, of Newcastle on Tyne. It was later bought by Scottish & Newcastle Breweries Ltd, who shipped the beer from Montrose to Newcastle. In 1957, it was acquired by Joseph W. Hobbs who then owned the Ben Nevis distillery and converted it into a distillery capable, like Ben Nevis, of producing grain and malt whisky with a patent still alongside the pot malt stills. In 1973 the large Spanish Company Destilerias y Crianza del Whisky S.A. of Madrid, known as DYC for short, acquired it, the first continental take-over of a distillery. They closed down the grain side and concentrated on producing highland malt whisky. The distillery had a capacity of a million proof gallons a year. Most went for blending in Scotland, although some went to Spain for use in blended Spanish whisky and some to the independent bottlers. Mothballed in the late 1980s it was acquired by Allied Distillers in 1994 and closed.

Owned by
Allied Distillers

Visitors
No

Age and strength when bottled
10 years old at 40% volume but mostly independent bottlings.

Comments
A smooth enough clean dry dram, it is a pity there are no plans to continue distilling or any prospective purchasers

LONGMORN

Situation
Elgin, Morayshire. Grampian Region

Classification
Highland (Speyside)

Origins and background
Two and a half miles south of Elgin near the village of
Longmorn, with a water supply from a never-failing local
spring and peat obtained from nearby Mannoch Hill, this
distillery was built in 1897 by John Duff at the height of the
whisky boom. In the same year he also built the neighbouring Benriach distillery, see Benriach. The controlling company was John Duff & Co. Ltd, but in 1898 James R. Grant
took over Longmorn, to be succeeded by his sons P. J. C.
Grant and R. L. Grant, trading as the Longmorn Distillery
Co. The Grants of Longmorn and the Grants of Glen Grant
were finally united in 1970 when Hill Thomson & Co. Ltd,
noted whisky blenders and merchants of 45 Frederick Street,
Edinburgh, where they had been trading since 1799, and
Longmorn-Glenlivet Distillers Ltd, merged with The Glenlivet and Glen Grant Distilleries Ltd, under the banner of The
Glenlivet Distillers. (See The Glenlivet.) Only eight years
later, in 1978, they were acquired by Seagram Distillers plc,
thus ending a proud record of independent and dedicated
Scottish control.

Owned by
Seagram Distillers plc

Visitors
No.

Age and strength when bottled
15 years at 45% volume

Comments
This used to be one of the very finest malt whiskies when
bottled at 10 years and 40% volume, very pale, with a clean
and delicate aftermath making it an excellent dram before or

after dinner. Then it ceased to be bottled except for the French market. Happily it is now bottled again, but at 15 years, no doubt to fit in with a marketing policy of having different malts available covering a range of ages. A victim of rationalisation it is now rather darker coloured and with the delicacy and fragrance it formerly had perhaps slightly masked. It is still however a good dram to drink at any time.

LONGROW *see* SPRINGBANK

MACALLAN

Situation
Craigellachie, Banffshire. Grampian Region

Classification
Highland (Speyside)

Origins and background
The distillery was first licensed legally on the Macallan's farm above a well known ford over the river Spey and the famous rock of Craigellachie in 1824, but there can be little doubt that illicit distilling had been carried on there for a number of years previously. This was a natural crossing on the Spey for the travelling cattle drovers who would generally spend a night at the farm, where it was reasonable that they would drink quantities of illicitly distilled whisky. They were also the obvious middle-men between the merchants in the south and the illicit distillers in the north, hence the Macallan farm was ideally placed for illicit trade. As with The Glenlivet, the reputation of the whisky immediately after the legal licensing of the distillery was already too widespread to account for its popularity in the south in any other way. The Macallan, like The Glenlivet, was off to a head start when the 1823 Act came into being in 1824. Nevertheless the distillery changed hands several times in the course of the 19th century before James Stuart sold it to Roderick Kemp in 1892. Kemp had been trained as a distiller at Talisker and soon began to improve Macallan.

By the time Kemp died in 1909 Macallan was already regarded as one of the finest Speyside malts. On his death a trust was formed for his two married daughters, their progeny and their descendants, still prominent shareholders. In 1950 a steady programme of modernisation and rebuilding was introduced over a six-year period, and in 1959 further rebuilding work was carried out. Finally in 1964 a second distillery was built alongside the old one and came into production in 1966 as an integral unit with the old. In 1996 an unexpected combination of minority shareholders resulted in a take-over by The Highland Distillers Ltd., who in turn were acquired by the Edrington Group in 1999, so that it still remains in Scottish hands.

Production is now around the one and a half million gallon mark a year, but remains in very high demand as one of the outstanding Highland malts. It may be that the distillery's insistence on the use of small stills similar to the originals and never using caramel for colouring, but always maturing the spirit in sherry casks, and achieving a standard colouring by blending whiskies from different casks are amongst the secrets of their outstanding success. Certainly this is a classic case where Scottish distillers so far unhampered by transatlantic take-overs, or accounting methods, or love of standardisation and modern marketing theories have proved themselves infinitely superior by using to the full the old methods and the well tried and tested principles of pot still malt whisky distilling. The malt whisky is marketed as The Macallan.

Owned by
The Macallan Distillers Ltd

Visitors
All year by arrangement.Tel: 01340 810221 Fax: 01340 870262

Age and strength when bottled
10 year old at 40% volume; also 12 and 18 years at 43% volume and 25 years at 43% volume

Comments
If only the success of this fine malt whisky could be a lesson to those transatlantic or foreign conglomerates who now own other well-known malt distilleries. In any shape and form The Macallan is a joy to drink, with an initial sweetness, but smooth body and splendid aftermath and it can only be said that as it ages it improves. It is well marketed and deservedly popular.

MACDUFF

Situation
Banff, Banffshire. Grampian Region

Classification
Highland (Speyside)

Origins and background
This distillery, which draws its water for cooling from the nearby river Deveron, was built near Banff in 1962 by a group including Brodie Hepburn Ltd. In 1972 William Lawson Ltd, bottlers, blenders and whisky merchants based in Coatbridge bought it and expanded it to four stills. Capacity is now around 750,000 proof gallons. In 1980 they became part of the General Beverage Corporation of Luxembourg, a subsidiary company of Martini Rossi. They in turn were acquired by Bacardi Ltd in 1991, who operated the distillery through William Lawson. When John Dewar & Sons were acquired by Bacardi Ltd in 1998 William Lawson and the distillery became part of the group. The single malt called **Glen Deveron** is readily available and well marketed. Some, however, is bottled by the independent bottlers as Macduff.

Owned by
John Dewar & Sons Ltd.

Visitors
Reception centre. Open most of the year: Tel: 01261 812612 Fax: 01261 818083

Age and strength when bottled
10 years at 40% volume

Comments
A good straightforward Speyside after-dinner malt whisky, clean tasting with a dry and pleasing aftermath.

MANNOCHMORE

Situation
Elgin, Morayshire. Grampian Region

Classification
Highland (Speyside)

Origins and background
This distillery was built by John Haig & Co. Ltd in 1971 about two and a half miles south of Elgin, alongside their malt distillery at Glenlossie and also drawing its water from the Bardon burn. It has a capacity of a million proof gallons, but most of the production goes for blending.

Owned by
UDV

Visitors
No

Age and strength when bottled
12 years at 43% volume

Comments
Like neighbouring Glenlossie still not widely available, but a welcome addition to the single malts. United Distillers wisely changed the DCL die-hard refusal to bottle and market their single malts. It is to be hoped UDV continue the policy.

MILTONDUFF

Situation
Elgin, Morayshire. Grampian Region

Classification
Highland (Speyside)

Origins and background
Built close to the famed Pluscarden Abbey ruins in 1824, almost certainly on the site of a previously illicit distillery, its' mash house is said to have been built on the old abbey brewhouse. The water from the Black Burn flowing from the peaty slopes of the Black Hill provides an ample water supply. Established by Messrs Bain and Pearey, it was soon transferred to William Stuart. During the early 1890s a good deal of renovation and rebuilding took place and by 1896 it was capable of producing 300,000 proof gallons a year. After the whisky boom, in common with all malt distilleries, it went through a long lean period then in 1936 it was sold to Hiram Walker. In 1975 it was modernised and enlarged so that with six stills it now has a capacity of two million proof gallons a year or over 5 million litres of alcohol. From the mid-1960's another malt whisky known as **Mosstowie** was produced from this complex using Lomond-type stills, (See Inverleven) but these were dismantled in 1981. Allied Distillers acquired the distillery in 1988 and it was modernised again in 1999.

Owned by
Allied Distillers

Visitors
By arrangement only: Tel: 01343 554139 or 01343 547433

Age and strength when bottled
12 years at 43% volume: 15 years at 46% volume

Comments
A very reasonable Speyside malt whisky, smooth and clean with a delicate aftermath, The 15 year old has altogether more body.

MORTLACH

Situation
Dufftown, Banffshire. Grampian Region

Classification
Highland (Speyside)

Origins and background
This distillery owes its name to the parish in which it lies. The Gaelic meaning of Mortlach is 'a bowl shaped valley' and the distillery stands in a hollow in the hills just outside Dufftown on the river Dullan, but draws its water from a locally famed Priests' well. Although undoubtedly based on the site of an earlier illicit still it was first licensed in 1824 to John Findlater. In the following year he took on two partners, Gordon and Mackintosh. By 1854 Gordon was the sole survivor and was joined in that year by George Cowie. Ten years later in 1865 George Cowie was the sole owner. Trading as George Cowie & Sons the company benefited from the whisky boom and in 1897 changed from three to six stills. After surviving the recession during the 1914-18 War it was acquired by John Walker & Sons Ltd, in 1923, thus passing to DCL control. It was totally re-built in 1964.

Owned by
UDV

Visitors
No

Age and strength when bottled
14 years old and 43% volume

Comments
A mellow Speyside malt whisky making a very pleasing after-dinner dram with a good aftermath.

MOSSTOWIE *see* MILTONDUFF

OBAN

Situation
Oban, Argyll. Strathclyde Region

Classification
Highland (Western)

Origins and background
In the 1960's Oban, one the smallest distilleries, also claimed to be the oldest in continuous production. It is said that distilling began in 1794, since when it has had a number of owners. In 1898 it was bought by the Oban and Aultmore Distilleries Ltd with the intention of acting as a major supplier to the notorious Pattison Ltd, of Leith whose bankruptcy in that year signalled the end of the whisky boom. It was indicative of the distillery's strength that it survived their failure and was only sold again in 1923, when a partnership bought it and formed the Oban Distillery Co. Ltd. In 1930 Scottish Malt Distillers Ltd acquired it and it became part of DCL. Closed in 1968, because it was felt its historic town-centre site was too small, it re-opened in 1972 with a new still-house and the two stills converted to internal steam heating after only a four year break.

Owned by
UDV

Visitors
Reception centre. Open all year round: Tel: 01631 572004 Fax: 01631 572011.

Age and strength when bottled
14 years at 43% volume

Comments
This is a very pleasing distinctive malt whisky with plenty of body and a good aftermath, possibly a little more like a Highland than a West Coast dram, but equally suitable for drinking before or after dinner. Another 'Classic Malt'.

OLD FETTERCAIRN *see* FETTERCAIRN

OLD PULTENEY *see* PULTENEY

PITTYVAICH

Situation
Dufftown, Banffshire. Grampian Region

Classification
Highland (Speyside)

Origins and background
Built in 1974 on the outskirts of Dufftown in the Dullan Glen by Arthur Bell & Sons Ltd, close to their other distillery, named after the town. The water for the distillery is drawn from the same two springs Balliemore and Convalleys. It has four stills, which are exact replicas of those in its older neighbour, and it operates in conjunction with the latter as part of the same distillery complex. Most of the production goes for blending but some is now bottled. Like Dufftown the distillery sometimes used the Glenlivet affix, for which there is surely no justification. Now part of UDV, it was closed in 1993.

Owned by
UDV

Visitors
No

Age and strength when bottled
12 years at 43% volume

Comments
A pleasing Speyside malt not surprisingly somewhat similar to Dufftown, but perhaps a little heavier.

PULTENEY

Situation
Wick, Caithness. Highland Region

Classification
Highland (Northernmost)

Origins and background
The fact that this is the only distillery in Caithness and the most northerly on the mainland emphasises the lack of good road and rail communication. It was established in 1826, not far from the ruined castle on the cliffs known as the Auld Man of Wick, one of the notable landmarks above the town. It has ample water supplies available from the Loch of Hempriggs. Peat is also no problem in a countryside where houses were frequently roofed with it. The distillery remained under control of the Henderson family until the 1920's slump, when it was acquired by James Watson & Co. Ltd., in 1923, part of DCL. It was then closed down in 1926 during the depression years and remained closed for a long period until 1951. By then it had been acquired by Mr R. Cumming but was in turn bought from him by Hiram Walker & Sons (Scotland) plc. In 1959 through their subsidiary J. & G. Stodart Ltd, they extensively renovated and modernised it with two stills. In 1995 it was acquired by Inver House Distillers. The bulk goes for blending, although some is bottled as **Old Pulteney**, but see below

Owned by
Inver House Distillers

Visitors
Reception centre. Tel: 01955 602371

Age and strength when bottled
8 years old at 40% volume

Comments
This is amongst the fastest maturing of the Highland malt whiskies. It is a full-bodied, peaty single malt and a good pre-dinner dram, but hardly merits the prefix Old.

ROSEBANK

Situation
Camelon, Falkirk, Stirlingshire. Central Region

Classification
Lowland

Origins and background
According to the Statistical Account for Scotland of the period, Messrs Stark Brothers were distilling at Camelon in 1798, but the forerunner of the present distillery complex was begun by James Rankine in 1840 and the site was originally chosen for its ready water supplies. In 1864 he was followed by his son R. W. Rankine who rebuilt the entire distillery and increased demand for the distillery's product greatly. In 1894 the Rosebank Distillery Ltd was formed as a public company and a second issue of shares in 1897 was immediately fully subscribed. However Rosebank was badly affected by the collapse of the whisky boom in 1900 and the slump that followed. In 1914 it was one of the companies which amalgamated to form Scottish Malt Distillers Ltd, becoming a subsidiary of the DCL and then of United Distillers plc. Unusual in that it was triple-distilled with one wash still and two spirit stills. It was closed in 1993.

Owned by
UDV

Visitors
No

Age and strength when bottled
12 years at 43% volume

Comments
A dry dram with a good flavour and plenty of body, it tastes more like a Highland than the Lowland malt whisky it is, possibly because of the triple distillation. It is no longer commercially available.

ROYAL BRACKLA

Situation
Nairn, Morayshire. Grampian Region

Classification
Highland (Northern)

Origins and background
The distillery was founded at Cawdor, close to Nairn, in 1812 by Captain William Fraser and received the prefix 'Royal' in 1835 at the command of William IV to show his approval of the whisky. Whether 'Silly Billy's' commendation was up to much is another matter, but it was the first distillery to gain a Royal warrant, renewed in 1838 under Victoria. The distillery changed hands a number of times before the Brackla Distillery Co. Ltd was formed in 1898 and bought the lease and more land from the Earl of Cawdor for expansion. In 1919 John Mitchell and James Leith of Aberdeen acquired the company and in 1926 sold it to John Bisset & Co. Ltd of Leith. In 1943 they were taken over by DCL. Subsequently in 1965 the distillery was modernised and expanded with four steam fired stills of 5,000 gallon capacity and a new malting. In 1998 control passed to Bacardi after a Monopolies Commission decision on the UDV merger. Most of the production goes for blending.

Owned by
John Dewar &Sons

Visitors
No

Age and strength when bottled
10 years old at 43% volume

Comments
A good pale, clean flavoured after-dinner dram with a pleasing slightly peaty aftermath.

ROYAL LOCHNAGAR

Situation
Crathie, Ballater, Aberdeenshire. Grampian Region

Classification
Highland (Eastern)

Origins and background
The distillery, only a mile from Balmoral, was built in 1845 beneath the mountain from which it takes its' name and its' water. In 1848 on 12th September Queen Victoria accompanied by Prince Albert and her young family toured the distillery, escorted by the founder John Begg, who persuaded them all to try a dram, for which service he duly received a royal warrant. The distillery was known for much of the 19th century as the Royal Lochnagar Distillery. The advertising slogan 'Take a peg of John Begg' was one of the earlier examples of the kind. John Begg was a considerable entrepreneur in his day and from Aberdeen initially set up a world-wide export and blending business finally based in Glasgow. On his death in 1880 his son Henry Begg continued the business as John Begg. In 1916 they were taken over by DCL and the Royal prefix was dropped for some time, but has since been resuscitated. Much of the production goes for blending, but some is bottled as the only surviving example of a Deeside malt whisky.

Owned by
UDV

Visitors
Reception centre. Open all year: Tel 013397 42700 Fax: 013397
42702

Age and strength when bottled***
12 years at 40% volume

Comments
A very pleasant smooth tasting fresh clean after-dinner dram with a good aftermath.

SCAPA

Situation
Kirkwall, Orkney

Classification
Island (Orkney)

Origins and background
In 1885 Mr J. T. Townsend, a Speyside distiller, built what was then a very advanced distillery two miles from Kirkwall, the capital of Orkney, on the north side of Scapa Flow and obtaining its water supplies from the Lingro Burn. It naturally has had very close connections during both world wars and after the First World War German Fleet was scuttled in full view of the distillery. The distillery itself had naval ratings billeted in it during the War and when fire broke out they helped to fight the blaze and save the distillery. After the War control was passed to the Scapa Distillery Co. Ltd, subsequently taken over by Bloch Brothers (Distillers) Ltd. In 1954 Hiram Walker & Sons (Scotland) plc acquired it as part of their plans for expansion and it was largely rebuilt in 1959. Acquired by Allied in 1988 and closed for a lengthy period it has been producing periodically under the management of Highland Park.

Owned by
Allied Distillers

Visitors
By arrangement. Tel: 01856 872071

Age and strength when bottled
10 years at 43% vol

Comments
A pleasing malt with a passing resemblance to the other Orkney, 'Highland Park,' but somewhat lighter and a good dram in its' own right. Good it is available again, even in limited quantities.

SINGLETON *see* AUCHROISK

SPEYBURN

Situation
Rothes, Morayshire. Grampian Region

Classification
Highland (Speyside)

Origins and background
Built in 1896, by the brothers John and Edward Hopkins, who in partnership with their cousin Edward Broughton, controlled the well-known whisky blending and marketing firm of John Hopkins & Company Ltd. There is a plentiful water supply from the Granty (Birchfield) burn, a tributary of the Spey. The distillery was first registered in the name of the Speyburn-Glenlivet Distillery Co. Ltd, but the Glenlivet affix is now discarded. In 1916 John Hopkins was taken over by DCL, but not totally integrated until 1931. The distillery has only two stills but was prominent in trying to overcome the problem of pollution in the River Spey. Most went for blending and is accepted as of high quality. It is now readily available. Acquired from United Distillers by Inver House in 1992.

Owned by
Inver House Distillers Ltd

Visitors
No

Age and strength when bottled
10 years at 40% volume

Comments
A pleasantly mellow Speyside dram which merits drinking at any time.

SPEYSIDE

Situation
4 miles s. of Kingussie at Drumguish

Classification
Speyside

Origins and background
In 1958 George P. Christie established the North of Scotland Grain distillery near Cambus, subsequently sold to DCL in 1984. From the 1950s he planned a malt distillery at Drumguish on the site of a 19th century mill where the river Tromie enters the Spey. Built in local stone by a single master stonemason, Mr Alexander Fairlie, over twenty years, it finally came on stream in 1990, with stills of half a million gallon capacity. It remains a family venture with George P.Christie still behind it. Currently marketed unaged as Drumguish and at 8 years old as 'The Speyside'.

Owned by
The Speyside Distillery Co., Ltd

Visitors
By arrangement: Tel: 0141 353 0110

Age & Strength when bottled
Drumguish, unaged at 40% volume. 'The Speyside' at 8 years and 40% volume.

Comments
It is good to see Scots bucking the trend towards ever-larger combines. Another example of a fast maturing malt whisky, the unaged Drumguish, a splendidly evocative name, is obviously young, but a good dram. Marketed as ' The Speyside' at 8 years it is a pleasing malt with a particularly good peaty aftermath.

SPRINGBANK

Situation
Campbeltown, Argyll. Strathclyde Region

Classification
Campbeltown

Origins and background
Springbank, established by the Mitchell family in the late 1820s, is one of the two distilleries left in Campbeltown once regarded as Scotland's whisky capital and the only one to have survived without closing. Chairman Mr Hedley Wright is great great grandson of the founder. Notable as the only Scottish distillery still conducting all its own operations from malting to bottling on site, the distilling process features an unusual method of re-distilling the feints in what amounts to a two and a half times distillation. Also notable for producing three different single malts. As well as Springbank, it very occasionally produces another single malt named **Longrow**. This is distilled with only peat-dried malted barley making it much heavier as a result. It also now produces the triple-distilled **Hazelburn**. The distillery has three times won the Championship Award at the Wine & Spirit Fair at Ljubljana in Yugoslavia.

Owned by
J. & A. Mitchell & Co. Ltd

Visitors
By arrangement. Tel: 01586 552085

Age and strength when bottled
10 and 21 years at 46% volume

Comments
Springbank is interesting and distinctive, reminiscent of an Irish whiskey with an initial sweetness and a pleasing aftermath, making a very satisfying dram. Longrow at 10 years and 46% is more like a smooth west-coast malt, reminiscent of an Islay dram with a long aftermath. Hazelburn in production for only three years will not be mature until 2008.

STRATHISLA

Situation
Keith, Banffshire. Grampian Region

Classification
Highland (Speyside)

Origins and background
In 1786 a Mr George Taylor obtained a charter from the Earl
of Findlater and Seafield for a distillery on the site, thus
making this one of the earliest operating distilleries in the
Highlands. From around 1830 it was owned and managed
by William Longmore and his successors, initially as the
Strathisla distillery and latterly as the Milton distillery, a
name still used by some locals. In 1950, still a private
company, it was acquired by Chivas Brothers Ltd, themselves a subsidiary of Seagram Distillers plc, who promptly
changed the name back from Milton to Strathisla and added
the hyphenated Glenlivet affix, although a considerable
distance from the Livet. While still adding the affix to the
distillery it has now been dropped from the label on the
bottle. Strathisla, in fact, obtain their water supplies for
cooling from the River Isla and for distilling from a reservoir
filled by a spring in the hills. On the other side of the River
Isla stands the sister distillery, Glen Keith (another that used
to add the Glenlivet affix) which was built in 1958. Most
went for blending but some was bottled by Chivas Brothers
and the independent bottlers. It is now widely available.

Owned by
Seagram Distillers plc

Visitors
Reception centre. Tel: 01542 783044

Age and strength when bottled
12 years and 43% volume

Comments
Like Glen Keith now readily available and a pleasantly
smooth medium-bodied dry after-dinner dram.

STRATHMILL

Situation
Keith, Banffshire. Grampian Region

Classification
Highland (Speyside)

Origins and background
Originally called the Glenisla-Glenlivet Distillery, Strathmill was built on the site of a former flour mill in 1891 and was acquired by W. & A. Gilbey in 1895 at the height of the Scotch whisky boom. Initially they marketed malt whisky only, but then turned to blending and marketed their noted blend Glen Spey. In 1962 they merged with Gilbey Twiss, Justerini & Brooks and United Vintners to form the International Distillers & Vintners, now part of UDV. The output of the distillery is all used for blending.

Owned by
UDV

Visitors
By arrangement

Age and strength when bottled
None bottled by the distillery

Comments
An independent bottling at 11 years and 60% vol tasted smooth with a slightly sweet flavour and aftermath.

TALISKER

Situation
Carbost, Isle of Skye

Classification
Island (Skye)

Origins and background
First established in 1830 the distillery was twice moved before settling where it now sited on the shores of Loch Harport. Its water for cooling is obtained from the nearby Carbost Burn. In 1898 the Talisker Distillery Ltd, amalgamated with the Dailuane-Glenlivet Distillery Ltd, which resulted in the formation of Dailuane-Talisker Distilleries Ltd, which also controlled the Imperial-Glenlivet Distillery close to Dailuane. The three distilleries in this group were acquired in 1916 jointly by Dewar, DCL, W. P. Lowrie and Johnnie Walker. In 1925 at the time of the great amalgamation which saw Dewar and John Walker both absorbed into DCL they also became part of DCL and since then have been controlled by Scottish Malt Distillers, although for many years the three were run as a separate company.

Owned by
UDV

Visitors
Reception centre. Open all year: Tel: 01478 614308 Fax: 01478 614302

Age and strength when bottled***
10 years at 45.8% volume

Comments
A very smooth and pleasing distinctive and unmistakeably west coast malt whisky with a full body and strong aftermath making a notable after-dinner dram. Another of United Distillers six 'Classic Malts'.

TAMDHU (*tamdoo*)

Situation
Knockando, Morayshire. Grampian Region

Classification
Highland (Speyside)

Origins and background
Yet another of the many distilleries built around the time of the Scotch whisky boom years, Tamdhu was established in 1897. The Gaelic meaning of Tamdhu is 'small black hill' and it is under just such a hill that the distillery lies on the banks of the Spey. In 1898 the controlling company Tamdhu-Glenlivet Ltd was acquired by the Highland Distillers Ltd, although operating as a separate subsidiary. Like many others the distillery was shut down for a long period from 1927 to 1948. Renovated and modernised in the 1970's, with six stills, but now discarding the Glenlivet affix, it is another useful asset amongst the distilleries acquired by the Edrington Group in 1999.

Owned by
Highland Distillers Ltd.

Visitors
No

Age and strength when bottled
Unaged at 40% volume

Comments
A sound, full-bodied malt whisky with a good mellow aftermath making a pleasing after-dinner dram. It is well marketed and readily obtainable.

TAMNAVULIN–GLENLIVET
(*tamnavoolin*)

Situation
Ballindalloch, Banffshire. Grampian Region

Classification
Highland (Speyside)

Origins and background
The Gaelic meaning of Tamnavulin is 'the mill on the hill' and near to the site of this distillery are the ruins of an old mill. It was built by the Invergordon Distillers Ltd in 1966 on the west bank of the river Livet at the base of the Cairngorm mountains. It is among the few distilleries which is entitled to use the hyphenated affix Glenlivet with good reason. Acquired by Whyte & Mackay in 1993 and currently moth-balled.

Owned by
JBB (Greater Europe) plc

Visitors
No.

Age and strength when bottled***
10 and 12 years at 40% volume

Comments
A light, slightly peaty, typical smooth Speyside malt whisky with a good aftermath making a pleasing dram at any time.

TEANINICH

Situation
Alness, Ross-shire. Highland Region

Classification
Highland (Northern)

Origins and background
Facing the Cromarty Firth this distillery probably dates back
to the 18th century. Some of the original buildings put up by
Captain H. Munro of Teaninich in 1817 are still visible today.
The distillery is close to the River Averon but its water comes
from the Dairywell spring. In 1895 two partners named
Munro and Cameron took over the distillery and acquired
the lease from the Munro family. In 1905 on his partner's
death Robert Innes Cameron took over the entire operation.
In 1933 his trustees sold out to the DCL. In the 1962 after
complete rebuilding and renovation the number of stills was
increased from two to four and in 1970 a new distillation unit
with six still was added. It part closed for some years in the
1980s and all the production then went for blending. Some is
now bottled.

Owned by
UDV

Visitors
No

Age and strength when bottled
10 years and 43% voilume

Comments
Even if in restricted supply it is good to have this satisfactory
single malt available once again.

TOBERMORY

Situation
Tobermory, Mull, Argyll.

Classification
Island (Mull)

Origins and background
Dating from about 1800 the distillery was bought by John Hopkins & Co. Ltd, around 1890. In 1916 it was acquired by DCL, but closed in 1928 and used as a store and electricity generating station, which is still working. In 1972 a Liverpool Shipping Company completely rebuilt and re-equipped it and with Spanish and Panamanian backers formed a company called the Ledaig Distillery (Tobermory) Ltd. It was then bottled as Ledaig. In 1975 the company closed down having just raised the distillery's capacity to 800,000 litres a year with four stills. In 1976 a Receiver was appointed and in 1979 the Kirkleavington Property Co. of Cleckheaton, Yorkshire, took over, operating as the Tobermory Distillers Ltd. Most went for blending, but some was available as a single malt. It was closed in 1981, but distilling started again in 1990. In 1993 it was acquired by Burn Stewart and in 1994 began producing both Tobermory, using unpeated malted barley, and Ledaig, using heavily peated malted barley.

Owned by
Burn Stewart Distillers plc

Visitors
Open from Easter to September: Tel: 01688 302 647

Age and strength when bottled
Tobermory at 10 years at 40% and 43% volume: Ledaig, unaged at 42% volume:

Comments
Tobermory is perhaps more like a Speyside malt than a west coast island product, but a good dram by any standards. Ledaig, although young, is at once recognisable as a west coast dram with a strong peaty aftermath.

TOMATIN

Situation
Tomatin, Inverness-shire. Highland Region

Classfication
Highland (Northern)

Origins and background
About thirteen miles south-east of Inverness, at around the 1,028 foot level this distillery is amongst the highest, although close to the main road and the railway. Established in 1897 by the Tomatin Spey District Distillery Co., Ltd., up to the outbreak of the Second World War it was eminently successful. On resuming distilling after the War the distillery was producing 120,000 proof gallons a year from its two pot stills. After successive programmes of modernisation by 1975 the number of stills was increased to 23 with a capacity of 5 million proof gallons. A high degree of automation and the latest methods were introduced throughout the entire distilling process, so that only a small workforce was required, despite the size of the operation. Water for the distilling process is obtained from the Monadhliaith Mountains via a local burn the Alt-na-Frithe, which flows into the River Findhorn. In 1985 the company went into liquidation and in 1986 was acquired by the Takara Shuzo consortium, the first malt distillery to be taken over by Japanese interests. Most goes for blending, some is exported in bulk and some bottled for export, but it is readily available in the U.K.

Owned by
Tomatin Distillery Co. Ltd.

Visitors
Reception centre. Open all year. Tel: 01808 511234 Fax: 01808 511373

Age and strength when bottled
10 years at 40% volume

Comments
A medium smooth, rather bland, but sound, pre-dinner dram.

TOMINTOUL (*tomintowl*)

Situation
Ballindalloch, Banffshire. Grampian Region

Classification
Highland (Speyside)

Origins and background
This modern distillery was established in 1965 by two firms of Glasgow whisky brokers, Hay & MacLeod & Co. and W. & S. Strong & Co., because of the shortage of malt whisky available for blending at that time. They chose a site some five miles north of Tomintoul close to the Glenlivet area justifying using the affix and with a plentiful supply of water from the Ballantruan Spring. Later additions brought the total capacity up to a million proof gallons, or 2.52 million litres of alcohol, a year with storage on the spot for two and a half million gallons, or 6.3 million litres of alcohol. The founder firms of whisky brokers subsequently merged with Whyte & Mackay Ltd. They were thus acquired by Jim Beam Brands, USA, through their subsidiary JBB(Greater Europe)plc. who sold the distillery in 2000 to Angus Dundee Distillers plc., whisky merchants, bottlers and blenders, wishing to expand. Most of the production goes for blending, but some is bottled.

Owned by
Angus Dundee Distillers plc

Visitors
Welcome by arrangement: Tel: 01807 590274

Age and strength when bottled
12 years at 40% volume

Comments
A very light and smooth pre-dinner dram with a good aftermath.

TORMORE

Situation
Advie, Grantown-on-Spey. Grampian Region

Classification
Highland (Speyside)

Origins and background
Built in 1959 by Seager Evans & Co. Ltd this was the first completely new distillery to be built on Speyside this century. It was built to a totally new design by a past President of the Royal Academy, Sir Albert Richardson. It was a complete breakaway from traditional designs and consists of a distillery, warehouses and cooperage, as well as houses for the distillery workers, all built in Kemnay granite. Ample water supplies are available supposedly from the nearby Loch an Oir, which in Gaelic means Loch of Gold. Much of the product is used for blending but some is bottled for the distillery. In 1990 acquired from Long John International Ltd, by Allied Distillers Ltd.

Owned by
Allied Distillers

Visitors
By arrangement. Tel: 01807 510244

Age and strength when bottled
10 years at 40% volume: 15 years at 46% volume

Comments
The 10 year old is a fairly typical clean Speyside malt whisky with a pleasant aftermath making a satisfactory if rather light pre-dinner dram. The 15 year old has much more body and a longer interesting aftermath.

TULLIBARDINE (*tullibardeen*)

Situation
Blackford, Perthshire. Highland Region

Classification
Highland (Southern)

Origins and background
The distillery stands on the site of a 17th century Blackford Brewery in a hollow beneath the Ochil hills and takes its name from the moor of Tullibardine on which the nearby Gleneagles Hotel was built. The plentiful supplies of particularly good water for brewing ale for which the old brewery at Blackford was noted are now utilised by the distillery. The distillery was designed by Mr W. Delme Evans in 1949 for Wm S. Scott Ltd, but was acquired by Brodie Hepburn Ltd, and subsequently sold to Invergordon Distillers Ltd, in 1972. Two years later in 1974 after considerable rebuilding the distillery's capacity was doubled. Most is used for blending, but some is also bottled as a single malt. In 1993 acquired by Whyte & Mackay now part of Jim Beam Brands (Greater Europe) plc and currently mothballed.

Owned by
JBB (Greater Europe) plc

Visitors
No.

Age and strength when bottled***
10 years at 40% volume

Comments
This is light, fresh and clean, more resembling a Lowland malt whisky perhaps, but with a good aftermath and making a pleasant pre-dinner dram.

Highland
Lowland - and Island

Recent Closures

In recent years the following distilleries have irrevocably closed, but occasional bottles may still be available through independent bottlings or as a UDV Rare Malt.

Banff (Banff, Banffshire. Grampian Region)
Closed in 1983 and demolished by DCL.

Ben Wyvis (Invergordon, Highland Region)
Built next to the grain complex in 1965 and dismantled by Invergordon Distillers in 1975.

Convalmore (Dufftown)
Built in 1894. Closed by DCL in the 1980s and now used for storage by Wm Grant & Sons.

Dallas Dhu (2 miles south of Forres. Grampian Region)
Closed by United distillers in 1983 and reopened as a museum showing the workings of a traditional distillery.

Glen Albyn (Inverness. Highland Region)
Closed by DCL in 1983 and since demolished.

Glenlochy (Fort William, Highland Region)
Closed by DCL in 1983 and subsequently dismantled and sold by United Distillers.

Glen Mhor (Inverness. Highland Region)
Next to Glen Albyn also demolished by DCL.

Glenugie (Peterhead, Aberdeenshire. Grampian Region)
The most easterly distillery it was closed by Long John International in 1982 and the machinery sold for scrap.

Glenury Royal (Stonehaven, Grampian Region)
Closed by DCL in 1985 and sold for development in 1992.

Kinclaith (Near Glasgow. Strathclyde Region)
In operation for only 18 years, the distillery was dismantled in 1975 by Long John International.

Ladyburn (Girvan)
Built by Wm Grant & Sons next to the grain complex in 1965. It was dismantled in 1975.

Millburn (Inverness. Highland Region)
Closed and dismantled in 1985 by DCL the site is now occupied by a restaurant.

North Port (Brechin, Grampian)
Closed by DCL in 1983 and subsequently dismantled and sold by United Distillers.

Port Ellen (Port Ellen, Islay)
This distillery was closed in 1983 by DCL and is soon to be dismantled by UDV.

St Magdalene (Linlithgow, West Lothian. Lothian Region)
Closed down in 1983 by DCL, the site was developed into flats.

Some Notable Vatted Malts

ASDA, well-known High Street supermarkets sell Glen Shira Vatted Malt.

Berry Bros & Rudd, Ltd, well known 17th century St. James's Street wine merchants, even better known for their world famous Cutty Sark blend, also market Berry's All Malt.

Bulloch Lade, Ltd, part of UDV, market the well known Glen Ila Vatted Malt.

Burn Stewart Distillers Ltd market Glen Blair Pure Malt.

Chivas Brothers, well-known subsidiary of Seagram, market **The Centenary, 100 Malts**

Cockburn & Campbell, Ltd., of London, market their Special Malt.

Invergordon, a subsidiary of **JBB (Greater Europe) plc** market Sheep Dip 8 Years Old Pure Malt. (The Original Oldbury Sheep Dip.)

Matthew Gloag market Famous Grouse 10 yr old malt. (The Macallan, Highland Park and others)

Gordon & McPhail, of Elgin, market Old Elgin Malt, Pride of Islay 12 yrs old, Pride of the Lowlands 12 yrs old, Pride of Orkney 12 years old, Pride of Strathspey 12 yrs old.

JBB (Greater Europe) plc European subsidiary of Jim Beam Brands (Worldwide) sell unaged Corriemhor

Hedges & Butler, a subsidiary of Peter Russell, market Hedges & Butler Royal Malt.

Justerini & Brooks, Ltd, founded in the mid-18th century, now part of UDV, market J & B 12 yrs old Exception, Vatted Malt available only in France.

Lombard Scotch Whisky, Ltd, based on the Isle of Man, buy their whisky in cask, then mature, vat, bottle and market: Lombard's 12yrs old Pure Malt, also, unaged: Anchor Bay (Light) Golden Harvest (Medium) Smoking Ember (Full)

Storm (Rich) and: Tidal Ebb (Islay): Harbour Lights (Spey-side) and Driftwood (Highland).

James Martin & Co., Ltd, owned by Glenmorangie plc., market Dalvegan Old Highland Malt 10'yrs old sold only inb Portugal.

John Milroy Ltd, of Greek Street, London, market Milroy's 8 yrs old Malt whisky.

Praban na Linne, Ltd., on the Isle of Skye, market Poit Dhubh, pronounced potch dhu, Gaelic for Black pot, an illicit still.

Peter J. Russell & Co., Ltd, of Edinburgh, market The Seven Stills 100% Malt 5 yrs old, and through their subsidiary William Maxwell, Ltd, Maxwell Malt.

Safeway, the supermarket chain, sells its own Safeway Special 12 Years Old Reserve Malt.

J. Sainsbury Ltd, the grocery supermarket chain, market Sainsbury's Highland Malt 12 yrs old.

Seagram Distillers, plc., market The Keith Classic.

Johnnie Walker, a subsidairy of **UDV** market Johnnie Walker Pure Malt 15 years old Vatted Malt.

UK Specialist Malt Whisky Sources

The following addresses of shops, stores and other sources specialising in Malt Whisky are all worth consulting or visiting, if the opportunity arises. As specialists in the field they are able to supply the extra knowledge, which may be lacking in the ordinary retail chain stores, however good their selection of malt whiskies may be. As specialists they will usually be able to find any malt whisky you may want and get it for you.

The Adelphi Distillery,
3 Gloucester Lane.
Edinburgh,
EH3 6AD.
0131 224 6670

Carley & Webb
29 Market Hill,
Framlingham,
Suffolk,
IP13 1AN.
0172 872 3503

Bloomsbury Wine & Spirit Co.,
3 Bloomsbury St.,
London,
WC18 3QE.
0207 236 4763

The Clifton Coffee House,
Tyndrum,
Crianlarich,
Perthshire,
FK20 KRY.
01838 400371

The Brighton Malt House,
1 North Road,
Brighton,
BN1 1YA.
01273 601060

Constantine Stores,
30 Fore Street,
Falmouth,
Cornwall.
01897 513295

Cadenhead Whisky Shop,
172 Canongate,
Royal Mile,
Edinburgh,
EH8 8DF.
0131 556 5864

The Covent Garden Whisky Shop
3 Russell Street,
London,
WC2 5JD.
0207 379 4640

Fortnum & Mason,
181 Piccadilly,
London,
W1A 1ER.
0207 734 8040

Gordon & MacPhail,
George House,
Boroughbriggs Road,
Elgin,
Moray,
IV30 1JY.
01343 545111

Peter Green & Co.,
Wine Merchants,
37 A/B Warrender Park Road.
Edinburgh,
EH0 1HJ.
0131 339 5925

Harrod's.
83–135 Brompton Road,
London,
SW1X 7XL.
0207 730 1234

Leith Mills' Whisky Shop
Bangor Road
Leith
Edinburgh
EH6 5JU
0131 553 5161

Loch Fyne Whiskies,
Inverary,
Argyll,
PA32 8UD.
01499 302219

Milroy's.
3 Greek Street,
Soho,
London,
W1A 1ER.
0207 437 0893

Robertsons of Pitlochry,
46 Athol Road,
Pitlochry,
Perthshire,
PH16 5BX.
01796 472 011

Royal Mile Whiskies,
379/381 High Street,
Edinburgh,
EH1 1PW.
0131 225 3383

Selfridges,
400 Oxford Street,
London,
W1A 1AB.
0207 730 1234

Strachan of Aboyne,
Balmoral Terrace,
Aboyne,
Aberdeenshire,
AB34 5HL.
013398 86121

The Vintage House,
42 Old Compton Street,
Soho,
London,
W1V 6LR.
0207 437 2592

The Whiskies, Cheese and Wine
Shop,
George Street,
Oban,
Argyll,
PA34 5NT.
01631 564409

The Whisky Castle,
6, Main Street,
Tomintoul.
Ballindalloch,
AB37 9EX.
01807 580213

The Whisky Shop,
3/2b, Waverley Shopping
    Centre,
Waverley Bridge,
Edinburgh,
EH1 1BQ.
0131 556 5688

The Whisky Shop,
Princes Square,
Buchanan Street,
Glasgow,
G1 3JX.
0141 226 8446

The Whisky Shop,
87 Bailgate,
Lincoln.
LN1 3AR.
01522 537 834

An Almanack of Distilling Dates and Events

An Almanack of Distilling Dates and Events

800 B.C.	Arrack known to have been distilled in India
584 B.C.	Aristotle born: later wrote of distilling in his Meteorology
A.D.432	St Patrick. A native of Scotland, sent to Wicklow to spread Christianity and also reputed to have introduced distilling.
1494	Entry in Exchequer Rolls regarding Friar Cor making aqua vitae from malted barley by order of the King.
1498	Lord High Treasurer's Account; 'To the barbour that brocht aqua vitae to the King in Dundee.'
1505	Barber surgeons in Edinburgh gained right of making aqua vitae.
1506	Treasurer's accounts in Inverness mention 'aqua vitae to the King.'
1527	The vertuose boke of Distyllacyon by Hieronymous Braunschweg published in English, translated by L. Andrew. First book on the subject, treated aqua vitae as a medicine.
1559	Treasures of Evonymous published by Peter Morwyng detailed methods of distilling process.
1579	First Act in Scotland specifically relating to Aqua Vitae.
1618	John Taylor in his Pennyless Pilgrimage visits the Earl of Mar and drinks aqua vitae. Earliest reference to 'uisge' being drunk at a Highland chieftain's funeral
1644	Charles 1 passed an Act of Excyse on 'everie pynt of aquavvytie or strongh watteris sold within the country.'
1655	R.Hage accused of distilling on the Sabbath in St. Ninian's Kirk sesssion records.
1675	Boyle re-discovered the principle of the hydrometer.
1690	Ferintosh first distillery mentioned by name. Forbes of Culloden who had 'suffered the loss of his brewery of aqua vitae by fire in his absence' in 1689 fighting for William of Orange against James was granted freedom from excise duty.
1707	Act of Union of Parliaments passed against much opposition, specifically excluded a tax on malt in Scotland.

1715	Attempt to introduce Malt Tax in Scotland withdrawn.
1725	Malt taxed in Scotland and riots resulted.
1726	In his Letters Captain Burt, an English engineer in the Highlands referred to the Highlanders drinking whisky 'like water.'
1736	Gin Act in England aimed at checking consumption caused open flouting of Law at height of Gin Era.
1745	Prince Charles raised standard at Glenfinnan.
1746	Prince Charles defeated at Culloden and fled country.
1747	Lt.Col.Watson in Fort Augustus advised his officers to get the Highlanders 'drunk with whisky.'
1751	An Act of Parliament specifically ended Scotland's exemption from taxation so that it was no longer advantageous to import spirits from Scotland.
1784	The Wash Act defined the Highland Line by Act of Parliament for Taxation purposes.
1786	Distillery Act introduced Licensing system at prompting of English gin lobby. Duty raised in Scotland to English level. No distinction between Highlands and Lowlands. This unfairness resulted in much illicit distilling.
1788	Duty increased. Stein brothers bankrupted.
1793	Tax on whisky trebled to £9.
1795	Tax on whisky doubled to £19. Some stills operated continuously to beat tax.
1797	Tax trebled to £54.
1800	Tax doubled again to £108.
1805	Tax raised yet again to £162. The firm of Seager Evans was formed in London to make gin.
1814	Stills under 500 gallons forbidden in the Highlands, which General Stewart of Garth said amounted to a complete interdict. Matthew Gloag set up as a whisky merchant in Perth.
1815	The output of the distillery at Drumin in Glenlivet run by George Smith grandson of John Smith Gow was already a hogshead a week. Due to the pure water and fine peat available the illicit whisky distilled there was regarded as the finest in Scotland and was drunk by many Highland lairds including Grant of Rothiemurchos MP and lawyer in Edinburgh.
1817	Teaninich distillery built by Captain H.Munro in Ross-shire.
1818	Bladnoch distillery founded near Wigtown by the Maclelland family.
1819	Clynelish distillery near Brora built by Marquis of Stafford.

1820	John Walker set up as a licensed grocer in Kilmarnock.
1821	Linkwood distillery near Elgin was built.
1822	George IV visited Edinburgh and was provided with illicitly distilled Glenlivet whisky from Grant of Rothiemurchos own cellar.
1823	A new Act introduced a £10 License fee and duty of 2s 3d per gallon of whisky distilled.
	Springbank distillery near Campbeltown founded by farmers named Mitchell.
1824	At the prompting of his landlord the Duke of Gordon George Smith took out the first license under the new Act as the first legal distiller in Glenlivet.
1825	T.R.Sandeman started as a whisky merchant in Perth.
1826	Robert Stein patented his single-distillation still
	Tax raised to 2s 10d per proof gallon. Tax per proof gallon raised to 3s 6d.
1830	Stein built his first patent-still at Kirkliston.
	Talisker was founded on the Isle of Skye.
1831	Aeneas Coffey invented his patent-still making grain whisky by continuous distillation.
	Justerini and Brooks went into partnership in London.
1832	The Glen Scotia distillery was founded in Campbeltown by Stewart Galbraith.
1836	The Glenfarclas distillery was founded by Robert Hay.
1838	Hill-Thomson whisky merchants granted a Royal Warrant.
1840	Glen Grant distillery built at Rothes by James and John Grant.
	Glenkinchie distillery founded in East Lothian by J. Gray.
	Tax per proof gallon raised to 3s 8d.
1841	James Chivas started as a merchant in Aberdeen.
1842	Glenmorangie distillery started at Tain by William Mathieson.
1846	John Dewar started as wine and spirit merchant in Perth.
1848	Queen Victoria and family visited John Begg at Lochnagar distillery.
1853	Andrew Usher credited with producing the first blended whisky.
	Gladstone raised the tax to 4s 8d per proof gallon.
1854	Crimean War. Tax raised to 6s per proof gallon.
1855	Tax raised to 8s per proof gallon.
1856	First Trade Arrangement by Grain Distillers.
	Tax raised by 1d per proof gallon.
1857	W & A. Gilbey set up as wine and spirit merchants.
	William Thomson joined William Hill and formed Hill

Thomson as whisky merchants at 45 Frederick Street, Edinburgh.

1860   Gladstone raised the tax per proof gallon to 10s.

1865   Glenfarclas distillery bought by James Grant of Blair-findy.

Whisky merchants Menzies, Barnard & Craig, John Bald & Co., John Haig & Co., MacNab Bros, and Mowbray and Macfarlane & Co., formed their first Trade Arrangement.

1870   Phylloxera Vastatrix began to attack the French vineyards.

1874   The North of Scotland Malt Distillers Association was formed.

1877   The Distillers Company Ltd.was formed by the whisky merchants who had formed a Trade Arrangement in 1865 with Menzies, Barnard & Craig replaced by Stewart & Co.

John Haig founded his company at Markinch in Fife.

1880   John Walker opened a London office. Colonel John Gordon Smith, son of George Smith went to court on the subject of the use of the name Glenlivet. It was held that he was the only one entitled to the name 'The Glenlivet.' Everyone else had to use it as an affix to their own distillery name.

1881   Bruichladdich Islay malt distillery was founded.

1882   William Sanderson produced his blend 'Vat 69'.

James Whyte and Charles Mackay founded Whyte & Mackay Ltd.

1884   James Buchanan set up in London with the blend 'Black & White'.

William Shaw at Hill Thomson produced the blend 'Queen Anne.'

1886   DCL shares quoted on London Stock Exchange.

1887   The Glenfiddich distillery built by William Grant.

The Dufftown-Glenlivet distillery founded.

Highland Distilleries was formed to acquire the Islay distillery of William Grant and the Glenrothes-Glenlivet distillery.

1888   The North British grain distillery founded with a productive capacity of 3 million gallons per annum. in opposition to the growing power of the DCL.

Mackie & Co., took over the Lagavulin distillery on Islay for White Horse.

1891   The Balvenie distillery founded by William Grant of Glenfiddich.

1893   Cardow was bought by John Walker.

1894   Longmorn-Glenlivet was built by Longmorn Co.

1895	Aultmore was built by Alexander Edward of Sanquhar, Forres.
1896	John Dewar built a distillery at Aberfeldy.
1898	The Pattison brothers went bankrupt ending the whisky boom.
1900	The tax per proof gallon was raised to 11s.
1906	The Islington Borough Council brought the 'What is whisky?' case. Basically malt v. grain. DCL pressed for Royal Commission when verdict in favour of malt.
1908	A Royal Commission on Whisky decided grain and malt blended made Scotch whisky.
1909	Lloyd George raised the tax per proof gallon to 14s 9d.
1914	First World War
	Scottish Malt Distillers formed as DCL subsidiary.
1915	Central Liquor Control Board formed.
	Immature Spirits Act required 2 years compulsory bonding.
1916	Compulsory bonding extended to 3 years.
1917	Dilution of Proof to 30 under proof.
	Whisky Association founded.
1918	War ended. Bonar Law increased tax by 15s 3d to 30s.
1919	Chamberlain increased tax per proof gallon to 50s.
1920	Prohibition introduced in U.S.A.
1924	John Walker merged with DCL.
1920	Chamberlain increased tax per proof gallon to 72s 6d.
1925	Buchanan-Dewars and John Walker merged with DCL with William Ross of DCL as Chairman.
1926	The Pot-Still Malt Distillers Association was formed in place of the North of Scotland Malt Distillers Association to include all malt distillers.
1927	Seager Evans set up Strathclyde distillery for grain whisky.
	White Horse Distillers was acquired by the DCL.
1928	The Distillers Co. of Canada took over Seagrams and Sons.
1929	Wall Street crash and depression.
1930	Hiram Walker of Ontario acquired Glenburgie-Glenlivet.
1932	Prohibition repealed by President F D Roosevelt.
1933	Arthur Bell & Sons acquired the Blair-Athol and Dufftown-Glenlivet distilleries.
1936	Edward VIII abdicated. George VI succeeded.
	Hiram Walker acquired George Ballantine & Co., of Dumbarton, also Milton-Duff distillery.
	Arthur Bell & Sons acquired the Inchgower distillery near Fochabers
	Seager Evans acquired John Long.

1937	Seager Evans took over Glenugie distillery at Peterhead.
1938	Hiram Walker opened a £3 million grain distillery at Inverleven, Dumbarton.
1939	Second World War
	Tax per proof gallon raised by 10s to 82s 6d.
	Grain distilling halted, limited pot-still malt distilling permitted.
1940	Tax per proof gallon raised by 15s to 97s 6d.
1942	Tax per proof gallon raised by 40s to 137s 6d.
1945	End of 1939-45 War.
1947	Tax raised by 33s 4d to 190s 10d by Hugh Dalton.
1948	Tax raised by 20s to 210s 10d by Stafford Cripps
1950	Seagrams took over Strathisla distillery.
1952	George IV succeeded by Elizabeth II
	George & J.G.Smith Ltd., and J & J Grant Glen Grant Ltd, formed The Glenlivet & Glen Grant Distillers Ltd.
1954	Hiram Walker took over Glencadam distillery in Brechin and Scapa distillery in Orkney.
1955	Hiram Walker took over Pulteney distillery in Wick.
1956	Seager Evans were bought by Schenley Industries of New York, in turn owned by the Glen Alden Corporation.
1957	Seager Evans built Kinclaith distillery near Glasgow.
1958	Seager Evans built a new distillery at Tormore on the Spey, north of Grantown-on-Spey.
	Chivas Brothers Ltd., subsidiary of Seagram of Canada built Glen Keith distillery at Keith in Banffshire.
1959	Inver House, an American-owned Company, a subsidiary of Publicker Industries, Inc., built a new grain distillery by Airdrie and an associated Lowland malt distillery named Glenflager.
1960	The Scotch Whisky Association was incorporated to provide legal status in foreign courts.
	Glenfarclas distillery was doubled in size.
	Ledaig distillery was founded on Tobermory.
	Jura distillery started by Scottish & Newcastle Breweries, Ltd.
1961	The tax per proof gallon raised by 21s to 231s 10d.
1962	Seager Evans acquired Laphroaig.
	W & A Gilbey, Gilbey Twiss, Justerinia & Brooks and United Vintners formed International Distillers and Vintners, Ltd.
1964	The tax per proof gallon was raised to £12.87.
1965	The tax per proof gallon was raised to £14.60.
	Caperdonich and Benriach distilleries were rebuilt after having been silent for over sixty years.
	Invergordon Distillers Ltd was formed.

Robertson & Baxter, a subsidiary of the Edrington Group acquire Lang Brothers and Glengoyne distillery

1966   The tax per proof gallon was raised to £16.06.
Tamnavulin-Glenlivet distillery built by Invergordon Distillers Ltd on the banks of the river Livet.

1968   The tax per proof gallon was raised to £17.14 in March and to £18.85 in November.

1969   Glen Alden Corporation, who owned Schenley Industries, who owned Seager Evans was taken over by Rapid American Incorporated. The name Seager Evans was changed to Long John International, Ltd.

1970   The Glenlivet and Glen Grant Distilleries merged with Hill Thomson & Co., Ltd., and Longmorn-Glenlivet Distilleries, Ltd.
Amalgamated Distilled Products was formed with the Campbeltown Glen Scotia distillery and other interests. The Highland Distillers Co., Ltd., acquired Matthew Gloag Ltd. and the blend The Famous Grouse.

1971   Chivas Bros, the Scots subsidiary of Seagrams, began plans for a distillery in Glenlivet. Currency was decimalised in Britain.

1972   The Glenlivet & Glen Grant Distilleries Ltd rationalised their name to The Glenlivet Distillers Ltd.
The Pot-Still Malt Distillers Association of Scotland rationalised their name to the Malt Distillers Association of Scotland.
Watney Mann & Co. Ltd acquired International Distillers & Vintners Ltd.
Whyte & Mackay Distillers Ltd., Dalmore and Tomintoul distilleries acquired by Scottish & Universal Investments Ltd.

1973   Britain entered the European Economic Community.
With the introduction of VAT the duty on whisky was reduced for the first time since 1896.
Bladnoch distillery was sold by Inver House Distillers to Arthur Bell & Sons.
Grand Metropolitan acquired Watney Mann & Co., Ltd., hence International Distillers & Vintners, Ltd.
Braes of Glenlivet distillery started operations.

1974   The Glenlivet Distillers Ltd 150th anniversary since George Smith first took out a licence in 1824.
Centenary of the Malt Distillers of Scotland
Lonrho acquired Scottish & Universal Investents Ltd. hence Whyte & Mackay Distillers Ltd.
Pernod Ricard acquired House of Campbell and control of Aberlour distillery.
Whitbread acquired Long John International

Allt-a-Bhainne distillery started production for Seagram Distillers Ltd.

1976   Seagram Distillers Ltd. opened vatting and blending complex at Keith with a capacity of three and a half million gallons per annum.

1978   Seagram acquired The Glenlivet Distillers Ltd.

1980   Heineken acquired 20% of Tomatin plc.

1981   Ben Nevis distillery acquired by Long John International.

1982   Pernod Ricard acquired William Whiteley and control of Edradour distillery.
       Glenugie distillery dismantled and sold by Long John International.

1983   DCL closed 11 of their 45 distilleries including Banff, Benromach, Brora, Dallas Dhu, Glen lbyn, Glenochy, Glen Mohr,, North Port, Knockdhu, Port Ellen, and St Magdalene, Banff, Glen Mohr and Glen Albyn in Inverness were subsequently demolished.

1985   Invergordon Distillers acquired Mackinlay and control of Jura and Glenallachie distilleries from Scottish & Newcastle Breweries.

1986   Arthur Bell & Sons acquired by Guinness plc after a lengthy take-over battle.

1987   Tomatin distillery acquired by a Japanese consortium Takara Shuzo Okura & Co., Ltd.
       Glenallachie distillery closed
       Guinness plc acquires control of DCL after allegedly fraudulent transactions (for which M/D Saunders is subsequently gaoled) in bitter take-over battle with the Argyll Group. It is agreed that their HQ will be based in Scotland.
       Long John International re-named James Burroughs Distillers.
       Inver House Distillers acquire Knockdhu distillery from DCL.
       'The Keepers of the Quaich' was founded on the lines of a Mediaeval Guild to promote Scotch Whisky.

1988   The Nikka Company of Japan acquired Ben Nevis distillery from James Burroughs Distillers planning to restart distilling in 1990.
       Management buy-out at Invergordon Distillers
       Allied Distillers Ltd. was formed, when Allied-Lyons plc. acquired Hiram Walker along with George Ballantine & Son, William Teacher & Sons and Stewart & Son of Dundee.
       Dallas Dhu distillery re-opened as a museum.
       Whyte & Mackay sold by Lonrho to Brent Walker.

DCL is merged with Arthur Bell & Sons plc. and is renamed United Distillers plc. The Headquarters to remain in London despite repeated assurances to the contrary during the take-over and subsequently.

Control of Barton International plc, part of the Argyll Group, owners of Littlemill and Glen Scotia distilleries, passed to Schenley International (Canada) plc., but later, following a management buy-out, was renamed Gibson International plc.

Inver House Distillers acquire Knockdhu from United Distillers.

1989   Suntory holding in Macallan raised to 12%.

Remy Martin own 11% in Macallan.

Glenallachie distillery acquired by Pernod Ricard from Invergordon Distillers.

Ardbeg distillery re-opened by Allied Distillers and Imperial and Glentauchers acquired from United Distillers plc. to be re-opened.

Management buy-out at Morrison Bowmore Distillers, owners of Bowmore, Auchentoshan and Glengarioch distilleries. Suntory has 35% holding.

The Scotch Whisky Heritage Centre is opened in Castlehill, Edinburgh, with excellent audio-visual displays, showing the history of Scotch whisky and the various stages of the whisky distilling process. 58% owned by American Brands Inc., subsidiary of Jim Bean bourbon.

1990   Whitbread, owners of Long John International Ltd, James Burroughs Distillers, sell Tormore and Laphroaig distilleries to Allied Distillers, Ltd.

Seagram Distillers Ltd., sell 45 Frederick Street, Edinburgh, the group and Hill Thomson HQ since 1857, one hundred and thirty three years after it was established as their base.

Gallagher Tobaccos plc., a subsidiary of American Brands Inc., take over Whyte & Mackay.

Kininvie distillery comes on stream,

1991   Whyte & Mackay, subsidiary of U.S based Gallagher Group, gained 42% shareholding in Invergordon Distillers after a hard fought take-over battle.

Bacardi Ltd, take over Martini Rossi and acquire William Lawson and control of Macduff distillery. (Glen Deveron)

The Speyside distillery came on stream

Burn Stewart & Co, Ltd. of Glasgow acquire Deanston distillery from Invergordon for £2.1 million.

1992   European Economic Commission standards accepted. The standard size of bottle was changed from 75 cl to 70 cl. It had already decreed that Scotch whisky shall only be distilled and produced in Scotland. It must also be no less than 40% volume since at anything less it is impossible to check whether it has been distilled in Scotland.

Inver House Distillers buy the Speyburn distillery from United Distillers.

In his March budget Chancellor Norman Lamont raised the duty on whisky by 85p to £19.81 per proof litre. The Exchequer now receives £5.54 in duty for each 70 cl bottle of whisky sold in Britain.

1993   Whyte & Mackay Group acquire Invergordon Distillers for US based conglomerate American Brands Inc. which owns Gallagher Ltd.

Burn Stewart Distillers plc, acquire Tobermory.

Bladnoch closed by United Distillers and sold to Co-ordinated Developments, Ltd. Opens as a Heritage Centre.

Gordon & MacPhail acquire Benromach distillery from United Distillers. It is re-equipped and re-designed Tobermory comes on stream.

1994   Control of Morrison Bowmore passed to Suntory who now have a considerable stake in the industry in Scotland as well as Japan.

VAT is raised to 17.5% compounding taxation. Chancellor Kenneth Clarke raises duty on whisky by 26 pence a bottle in emergency budget despite protests from the industry.

Gibson International plc in receivership. Littlemill Glen Scotia and Loch Lomond distilleries taken over by Glen Catrine Bonded Warehouse, Ltd, and pass to holding company the Loch Lomond Distillery Co., Ltd.

Allied Lyons and Pedro Domecq join forces to form Allied Domecq., in merger estimated at £740 million. Destileria y Crienza, owners of Lochside distillery, in Montrose was a subsidiary of Pedro Domecq, control now passed to Allied Distillers, Ltd.

1995   Whyte & Mackay mothball Bruichladdich, Tamnavoulin and Tullibardine distilleries because of over-production following the 1994 tax increase.

Total tax returns from Scotch whisky fell by £37 million and Chancellor Kenneth Clarke realising that excessive taxation is self-defeating reduced the tax on Scotch whisky by 27 pence. The first acknowledgement by any government since 1824 that whisky was over-taxed but still not enough to reverse trends.

At the International Wine & Spirit competition held In

Bordeaux the first 'Distiller of the Year' trophy sponsored by Allied Domecq and open to distillers of all spirits was won by Morrison Bowmore.

Inver House Distillers acquire Pulteney distillery from Allied Distillers, subsidiary of Allied Domecq.

The Isle of Arran distillery at Lochranaza comes on stream at a cost of £1.2 million.

1996   Chancellor Kenneth Clarke reduces the tax on Scotch whisky by a further 26 pence.

Inver House Distillers acquire Balblair distillery from Allied Distillers.

The Macallan Distillers taken over by Highland Distillers by unexpected combination of minority shareholders.

1997   Chancellor Gordon Brown raises the tax on Scotch whisky by 19 pence.

Grand Metropolitan, (International Distillers and Vintners), and Guinness, (United Distillers), merge to form new group named Diageo.

Ardbeg distillery on Islay bought from Allied Distillers by Glenmorangie plc for estimated £7 million

1998   After protests by Allied Distillers and Seagrams to the Monopolies Commission about the merger, Diageo sells Dewars subsidiary, with Aberfeldy, Aultmore, Craigellachie, and Royal Brackla distilleries to Bacardi. Ltd., for an estimated £1.5 billion.

Diageo merges spirit subsidiaries United Distillers and International Distillers and Vintners to form, United Distillers and Vintners, known as UDV. Allied Distillers bottling plant at Dumbarton closed.

Inver House Distillers acquire Balmenach distillery from UDV.

Benromach distillery, bought from United Distillers and restored by Gordon & MacPhail of Elgin comes on stream.

Jim Beam Brands, owners of American Brands, and subsidiaries, including Whyte & Mackay decide to rationalise by forming Jim Bean Brands (Greater Europe) plc or JBB (Greater Europe) plc.

The Highland Distillers group and The Macallan is taken over by a Scottish consortium of private financial investment group Edrington, owned by the Robertson family, with 70%, combining with William Grant & Sons, with 30%. Under the Chairmanship of Ian Good of Edrington a new subsidiary is named The 1887 Co., the year Highland Distillers was formed and the year William Grant built Glenfiddich. This is a new Scottish investment in mainstream Scottish industry. It has some of the best names available in its' portfolio, including the Famous Grouse, and, with Berry Bros & Rudd, also Cutty Sark.

2000   Bladnoch Distillery Ltd., re-started limited distilling.

Carribean distillers Angostura increase their holding in Burn Stewart to 28% after they make their first operating profit since 1997.

Jim Beam Brands (Worldwide) Inc.'s UK subsidiary JBB (Greater Europe) plc. sells Tomintoul distillery to Angus Dundee Distillers plc.

Seagram become a likely subject for one of the next major take-overs with the Bronfman family, descendants of the original founder of Seagram, who prospered during Prohibition, and Allied Domecq expected to be among the prominent bidders.

Glossary

Diastase
: In the process of germination the embryo of the barley secretes diastase, which makes the starch in the barley soluble and breaks it down. This is then checked by drying.

Draff
: The grain left in the mash tun after the wort has been drawn off for distilling. It is widely used as cattle feed and is one of the by-products of the distilling process.

Drying shed
: With its typical pagoda-shaped ventilators the drying shed, where the malted barley is dried is one of the established features of the older distilleries in Scotland.

Feints
: This is the third part of the distilled spirit in the second distillation of the pot-still distilling process. It consists of the undesirable higher alcohols. They are generally re-distilled.

Foreshots
: These are the first part of the distilled spirit in the second distillation of the pot-still distilling process. They consist of the undesirable lower alcohols. The 'middle cut' which follows is the desirable spirit used to make malt whisky.

Highland Line
: Introduced by Act of Parliament in 1784 to define for tax purposes the difference between Highland and Lowland distillers. If the line was applicable today most of the Banffshire and Aberdeen distilleries would be considered Lowland.

Low Wines
: This is the product of the first part of the potstill distilling process. It is the product of the distilled wash. The feints and foreshots are generally added to this prior to the second distilling process. Malt Barley (or other grain) prepared for brewing or distilling by steeping, germinating and kiln drying.

Mash
: The dried malted barley is ground in a mill and then mixed with boiling water in a circular container known as the mash tun. The soluble starch is then turned into a sugary liquid called wort.

Middle Cut	The desirable spirit produced between the fore-shots and the feints in the post-still process. On-stream A distillery comes 'on-stream when distilling starts.
Patent-still	Also known as the Coffey Still after its inventor Aeneas Coffey. Also known as a continuous still, since it works continuously producing grain whisky, unlike the two separate operations of the pot-still.
Pot-still	A large, usually round-sided, copper vessel used for the distillation of malt whisky.There are two pot-stills required for the process. Firstly the wash still which produced low wines. Those are then distilled in the adjoining smaller spirit still which produces malt whisky.
Proof	This is the technical term by which the strength of the spirit produced is measured. One of the early methods used was tomix the spirit with gunpowder and light it. If the powder lit there was deemed to be enough spirit to allow it to do so and this was then known as 'proved.' If there was no flash the spirit was held to be too weak. Today using a Sikes Hydrometer the strength is accurately measured.
Proof Spirit	Under the 1952 Customs & Excise Act 'Spirits shall be deemed to be at proof if the volume of the ethyl alcohol contained therein made up to the volume of the spirits with distilled water has a weight equal to that of twelve-thirteenths of a volume of distilled water equal to the volume of the spirits, the volume of each liquid being computed as at 51 degrees Fahrenheit.
Saccharify	To convert into sugar. In the distilling process this arises between malting and mash tun when the diastase enzyme turns the starch in the grain into sugar.
Single whisky	Either malt or grain whisky produced by a single distillery.
Single-single	Either malt or grain whisky produced from a single distillation by a single distillery.
Uisge Beatha	The Gaelic for eau de vie or the water of life or 'strong waters.' Used to refer to spirit distilled from malted barley it was shortened to 'uisge,' or 'usky,' hence the origin of the word whisky.
Wash	The term used for the liquid obtained from fermented wort. This is used for the first pot-still distillation process, or for the patent-still.

Wort   The liquid drawn from the mash tun containing the sugar from the malted barley. With the addition of yeast it is then fermented prior to being distilled as wash

Zern, a   A Transatlantic term for a measure of Scotch malt whisky; a sufficient quantity taken after any sporting activity to repel any chill and induce reflective discussion of the day; hence, a Zernful.

Further Reading

Bell, Colin: *Scotch Whisky*: (Lang Syne Publishers: 1954)

Barnard, Alfred: *The Whisky Distilleries of the United Kingdom*: (Harper 1887)

Brander, Michael: *The Original Scotch*: (Hutchinson, 1974) *A Guide to Scotch Whisky*: (Johnston & Bacon 1975) *An Introduction to Scotch Whisky*: (Spurbooks 1982) *The Essential Guide to Scotch Whisky*: Canongate 1990) *The Original Guide to Scotch Whisky*: Gleneil Press 1995) *Brander's Guide to Scotch Whisky*: (Lyons & Burford. N.York 1996)

Bruce-Lockhart, Sir Robert: *Scotch*: (Putnam, 1959)

Cooper, Derek: *A Taste of Scotch* (Deutsch 1989) *A Guide to the Whiskies of Scotland*: (Pitman, 1981) *The Century Companion to Whiskies* (Century 1987) & Fay Godwin *The Whisky Roads of Scotland*: (Norman & Hobhouse 1982) & Dione Patullo: *Enjoying Scotch*: (Cassell 1980)

Daiches, David: *Scotch Whisky: Past & Present*: (Collins) *Scotch Whisky*: (Deutsch 1969) *Let's Collect Scotch Whisky*: (Jarrold)

Dunnett, Alastair: *The Land of Scotch* (S.W.A 1953)

Fleming, Susan: *The Little Whisky Book*: (Piatkus)

Greenwood, Malcolm: *A Nip Around the World*: (Argyll 1995) *Another Nip Around the World*: (NWP 1998)

Gunn, Neil. M: *Whisky and Scotland*: (Routledge, 1935)

Hallgarten, Peter: *Spirits & Liqueurs* (Faber & Faber 1979)

Hastings, Derek: *Spirits & Liqueurs of the World*: (Apple: 1984)

House, Jack: *The Pride of Perth: A History of Arthur Bell & Sons*: (Hutchinson Benham, 1976) with Theodora Fitzgibbon, S.Russell Grant, Donald Mackinlay, Hugh MacDiarmid, Bill Simpson & Anthony Troon: *Scotch Whisky*: (Macmillan, 1979)

Hume, James R: See Moss:

Jackson, Michael: *Malt Whisky* (Dorling Kindersley 1989) *The World Guide to Whisky*: (Dorling Kindersley) *A Guide to Scotch Whisky*: (1988)

Keegan, Alan: *Scotch in Miniature*: (Famedrame 1976)

Lamond. John: *Scotland's Malt Distilleries*: (Benedict Books 1989) With Robin Tucek: *The Malt Whiskies File*: (Canongate Books, 1995)

Laver, James: *The House of Haig* (1958)

Lord, Tony: *The World Guide to Spirits, Liqueurs, Aperitifs and Cocktails*: (Macdonald & Janes, 1979)

MacDonald, Aeneas: *Whisky*: (Porpoise Press 1950)

Mackie, Albert D: *The Scotch Whisky Drinker's Companion*: (Ramsey Head Press 1975)

MacLean, Charles. *Malt Whisky Almanac*: (Lochar 1986)

McDowall, R.J.S. *The Whiskies of Scotland* John Murray 1967)

Milroy, Wallace. *Malt Whisky Almanac*: (Lochar, 1986)

Moore, Graham: *Malt Whisky*: (Swan Hill 1998)

Morrice, Philip; *The Schweppes Guide to Scotch* (Alphabooks 1983) *The Whisky Distilleries of Scotland and Ireland*: (Harper)

Moss, Michael S. with James R.Hume: *The Making of Scotch Whisky*: (James & James)

Murphy, Brian: *The World Book of Whisky*: (Collins 1978)

Robb, J. Marshall: *Scotch Whisky* (W & R Chambers 1950)

Ross, James: *Whisky*: (Routledge, 1970)

Saintsbury, George: *Notes on a Cellar Book* (Macmillan, 1920)

Sillett, S.W: *Illicit Scotch*: (Beaver Books, 1965)

Simon, Andre: *Drink*: (Burke Publishing, 1948)

Skipton, Mark: *The Scotch Whisky Book*: (Hamlyn, 1930)

Smith, Gavin D: *Whisky, Wit & Wisdom*: (NWP 1999)

Targett, David and Raymond K.Ashton: *Scotch Whisky: Too Much or Too Little*: (Tomatin Distillers, Co, Ltd., 1981)

Taylor, Iain Cameron: *Highland Whisky*: (An Comunn Caidhealach, 1968)

Townsend, Brian: *Scotch Missed*: (NWP 1997)

Weir, Ronald B: *A History of the Pot Still Malt Distillers' Association*: (Elgin 1970)

Wilson, John: *Scotland's Malt Whiskies*: (Famedrame 1975) *Scotland's Distilleries: A Visitor's Guide*: (Famedrame)

Wilson, Neil: *Scotch & Water* (Lochar)

Wilson, Ross: *Scotch Made Easy*: (Hutchinson, 1959) *Scotch*: (Constable 1970) *Scotch, Its History and Romance*: (David & Charles 1973)

THE GLENEIL PRESS

Whittingehame,
Haddington,
East Lothian,
EH41 4QA

Tel/Fax 01620 860292

E-mail: gleneil.press@freeuk.com

Web site: www.gleneil.com

Visit our website! Find out how to join The Clan
Gleneil to obtain any book sold by the Gleneil
Press at a 20% reduction on the Retail Price and
read our regular updates on whisky.

NOTES